The Timeless Moment

Books By D. Bruce Lockerbie

The Timeless Moment
Who Educates Your Child?
A Man Under Orders
The Cosmic Center
The Apostles' Creed
The Liberatening Word
The Way They Should Go
Purposeful Writing
Major American Authors (general editor and coauthor)
The Macmillian English Series Books 10 and 12 (coauthor)
Patriarchs and Prophets
Billy Sunday

The Timeless Moment

Creativity and the Christian Faith

D. Bruce Lockerbie

Cornerstone Books
Westchester, Illinois

Library of Congress Catalog Card Number 80-65332
ISBN 0-89107-181-4

For Lory,
my wife,
the very Incarnation of Love

Contents

Introduction and Acknowledgments

When or how the ideas that find expression in this book first occurred to me I cannot tell. In conversation with colleagues and students at The Stony Brook School over a span of two dozen years? In contemplation of an unforgettable lecture given by the novelist Madeleine L'Engle? As a result of studying for confirmation in the Episcopal Church?

Perhaps it's easiest to say that a writer grows from book to book. Some years ago, in a book called *The Liberating Word: Art and the Mystery of the Gospel,* I followed a line of reasoning that began with Creation by the Creator and ended with the making of art by his creatures. Now I realize that the link between theology and the human imagination is more complex than I had then perceived. While preparing to teach T. S. Eliot's *Four Quartets,* I became aware of a relationship I had never before grasped: I saw that art can best be appreciated by someone who knows and understands—as Eliot most assuredly did—not only the Christian doctrine of Creation, but also Incarnation and Vocation. I came to understand that God the Creator *calls each of us, his creatures,* to share his inimitable and absolute powers of creativity by allowing us to give form and shape to those ideals by which we live. God summons us to take his gifts of Creation and, by offering them back to him, raise our vocation to the level of art.

By *art*, I want no one to assume that I mean exclusively that which we institutionalize for exhibition or performance in museums, galleries, theatres, or concert halls. Customarily, painting and sculpture, drama and dance, opera, oratorio, and symphonic music, along with literature, are designated as "the arts," to the exclusion of everything else. While it is true that my concentration may appear to be given to discussing these so-called "fine arts," I mean also to include a much more comprehensive range of human experience. Gardening, cooking, architecture, sport and recreation, politics and government, travel, family and other social conduct, correspondence, and even conversation may also be *art* when received as gifts from God, invested like the talents in Jesus' parable, and returned to the Giver in his praise.

My reflections on these matters, interweaving Creation, Incarnation, and Vocation with the making of art, were developed into a series of lectures. This series was first presented at Trinity College, Deerfield, Illinois, in September 1977, under the sponsorship of the Thomas F. Staley Foundation. The series has been given subsequently, in whole or in part, to audiences throughout the United States of America and also in Great Britain.

I am grateful to Dr. E. Beatrice Batson, chairman of the English Department at Wheaton College, Illinois, whose invitation to serve as Visiting Professor of English initially stimulated my close study of Eliot's poetry; to The Stony Brook School and its headmaster, Karl E. Soderstrom, for allowing me ample opportunity to prepare and deliver these lectures; to Jan P. Dennis, editor of Cornerstone Books, for his encouragement to publish this work, now expanded; and to Mary Rost, for her careful preparation of the manuscript.

D. Bruce Lockerbie
Stony Brook, New York

> . . . But to apprehend
> The point of intersection of the timeless
> With time, is an occupation for the saint—
> No occupation either, but something given
> And taken, in a lifetime's death in love,
> Ardour and selflessness and self-surrender.

T. S. Eliot
Four Quartets

A Theology of Pots and Poems

A few years ago, my family and I spent eight months traveling around the world. Before we left home, several people asked me what sights I most wanted to see. That was easy. To make my trip rewarding, I must see Mount Everest, the Taj Mahal, and the Parthenon; I also named the Garden Tomb. No doubt a psychologist could have a field day with that kind of Rorschach test—mountains, a monument to enduring love, a temple honoring the goddess of wisdom, and everlasting life!

Standing on a promontory in Nepal at sunrise, I see the first darts of light fall upon points of the sawtooth at the top of the planet. Slowly its gray looming shape turns pink, then orange, then crimson, then dazzling white, as the sun bursts upon the glaciers of the Gamesh Himal, of Annapurna, and of Everest itself. We are a hundred miles away, but I have seen the great mountain, and I am impressed.

A few days later, we pass through a reddish sandstone arch and behold the most famous tribute to human love, the exquisite Taj Mahal. The humorist Edward Lear wrote, "Henceforth let the inhabitants of the world be divided into two classes—them as has seen the Taj Mahal, and them as hasn't." Its brilliance, its colorful arabesques, its paradise setting—all these affect me. But mostly I am stunned by its size. Having seen so many models and miniatures of the Taj Mahal, I am expecting to see a finely wrought mausoleum, perhaps the size of a McDonald's. I am not prepared for minarets some 130 feet high and a dome over 200 feet! I take Lory's hand in mine and promise her a love-sign comparable!

We travel on and some months later climb the Acropolis, up the sacred way, and into precincts of the virgin goddess of wisdom. Across the rubble of broken marble and limestone outcropping stands one of the world's most remarkable architectural accomplishments. Built in the time of Pericles and Sophocles, the Parthenon represents—as does no other single structure—the spirit of its age. Ravished by Turks and Englishmen alike, the Temple of Athena keeps her ancient secret, a perfect symbol of the classic virtues—truth, beauty, goodness.

I think often of these splendors of nature and human nature, forever a part of my experience, yet now increasingly hidden by enveloping time. Viewing them at first meant little more to me than satisfying some quirk of curiosity, like scratching an itch of desire to see the Seven Wonders of the World; or perhaps it was merely a means of chalking up an unbeatable conversation opener: "When I was in Katmandu . . ." Now, however, I see in these sights a fascinating connection and a far purer and lasting significance. For in the vaults of my memory where these experiences lie stored, I find in them instances of that phenomenon known to us all and called by T. S. Eliot, in his *Four Quartets*, "the intersection of the timeless moment."

Eliot sees our lives in a constant turmoil of frenzy and motion—a scene he dramatizes in "The Hollow Men" as a daily meaningless circuit "round the prickly pear." In the rush of our secular-minded preoccupation with mere existence, the bizarre, the occult, the banal take possession of our lives. We become slaves to speculation and to titillating rumors headlining the supermarket weeklies:

> To communicate with Mars, converse with spirits,
> To report the behaviour of the sea monster,
> Describe the horoscope, harupiscate or scry,
> Observe disease in signatures, evoke
> Biography from the wrinkles of the palm
> And tragedy from fingers; release omens
> By sortilege, or tea leaves, riddle the inevitable
> With playing cards, fiddle with pentagrams
> Or barbituric acids, or dissect
> The recurrent image into pre-conscious terrors—
> To explore the womb, or tomb, or dreams; all these are usual
> Pastimes and drugs, and features of the press:
> And always will be . . .

So says Eliot in the *Four Quartets*. But while he admits that "men's curiosity searches past and future/ And clings to that dimension," Eliot also acknowledges that, at rare moments, our lives may become frozen in stop-film by a vision beyond any routine experience. It may be fragmentary—only the essence of a vignette, the merest glimpse of a natural scene, a fleeting reminder of an incident supposedly long-since forgotten—but it is sufficient to break through the seeming relentlessness of time and give a foretaste of timeless eternity.

The moment is transitory, but even so it carries with it an aura of something almost holy. To use the words of C. S. Lewis, we find ourselves "surprised by Joy," overcome by "an unsatisfied desire which is itself more desirable than any satisfaction." Such are my memories of Mount Everest, the Taj Mahal, the Parthenon. In them I find representations of reality; with them I also find urges to give universality to one's own experience, urges to frame out of the flux of one's own life something permanent.

We call the product of these compulsions *art*, by which we mean nothing less than our expressed desire to scale the highest peak, immortalize love, and worship both wisdom and beauty. For as the American novelist Willa Cather once told a young painter named Grant Reynard, "The crux of this whole art experience is in that word *desire*—an urgent need to *recreate* a vital life experience which wells up within and must find release in the writing." But to formalize our random and idiosyncratic vision, we need to circumvent the strictures of time. We need to find some means of holding onto our singular and timeless moment. For each of us, as for Willa Cather, art is "but a mould in which to imprison for a moment the shining and elusive element which is life itself—life hurrying past us and running away, too strong to stop, too sweet to lose."

And so we try. We take pen in hand, we pause before an empty canvas, we sit in contemplation before a block of stone, or muse with an instrument idly sounding notes or strumming chords. We hope, in due course, to find something that works, something to approximate the feelings locked within us. More often than not, we surrender to a realization that we shall never succeed, that the transcendent experience has eluded us; the ability to break through barriers of time and space and there recapture the meaning of that moment lies outside our ken. When this is so, we may come to agree with Eliot, that

> to apprehend
> The point of intersection of the timeless
> With time, is an occupation for the saint—

Surely that's discouraging enough! Few of us qualify—venerable, beatified, canonized—as saints. Instead, says Eliot,

> For most of us, there is only the unattended
> Moment, the moment in and out of time.

Eliot is here recalling a pathetic awareness familiar to many of us. In trying to reach and retain that "timeless moment"—with a photograph or a love letter or a song—we discover that it is mercurial and ephemeral. It resists every effort to possess it. "The unattended moment" never lasts. Even when we think that we have grasped it, Clyde S. Kilby reminds us, "the perfect moment of insight or experience that we long for and sometimes attain begins next moment to be a fading image."

What is art that it should be so elusive? What is this "timeless moment" forever slipping out of our grasp? What is this insistence upon permanence in a world of mutability and decay? Eliot concedes that "the timeless moment" may consist of little more than "hints and guesses." Nevertheless, there is something there, and that *something* Eliot calls "Incarnation."

These are only hints and guesses,
Hints followed by guesses; and the rest
Is prayer, observance, discipline, thought and action.
The hint half guessed, the gift half understood, is
Incarnation.

Art is form and substance, a crystallizing of sense impressions, a communion between matter and spirit. No work of art exists without expression, floating in boundless vacuums of the imagination. No work of art exists until its formlessness surrenders to the artist's control, until he takes those scattered elements of thought, idea, intuition, or emotion and embodies them in oils or tones or words. This is what we mean when we declare that all art is incarnational, an attempt—however abstract or fluid it may appear—to give flesh and form to an ideal, to rescue it from oblivion and turn it into a "timeless moment."

Art, moreover, is an assertion of values, "one of the means," says Aldous Huxley, "whereby man seeks to redeem a life which is experienced as chaotic, senseless, and largely evil." Art points to a vase of flowers, a country dance, monuments from a ruined civilization, or a mother nursing her infant and says, "These are important. Look closely and see here a fundamental truth about life." But to tell its truth, art needs no special setting. Too often in our time art has suffered the stigma of being classified as "fine art" and thereafter separated from ordinary human concourse. Too often in our packaged education—survey courses in "Art History" and "Music Appreciation"—we have conveyed the impression that art may be experienced only in palaces like the Louvre or the Metropolitan, Carnegie Hall or the Academy of Music. But art belongs not only in the *musée des beaux arts*, but also in our homes. Its history and our appreciation will be discovered not only in the hallowed galleries and concert halls we visit, but also in the furniture we select, the plants and shrubs we nourish, the clothing we wear, the television programs we watch, the books we read, the food we prepare, and the manner in which we serve it—in short, the character of our discourse and the nature of our living. For where there is dignity, grace, and order, there is art.

Above all, art is humanity's badge of identification, signifying mankind's uniqueness among all the creatures of this cosmos. For let it be clear from the outset of this book that I speak from the vantage of one who believes that we are inhabitants of a created universe; I believe that the Creator is a God whom we can come to know in a personal relationship; that, furthermore, this God endowed each atom of his Creation with the need and capacity to reproduce itself, to "be fruitful and increase" (Genesis 1:22). But, my reading of Genesis tells me, this Creator-God gave to one creature only certain attributes and responsibilities not common to the rest of Creation.

Of man, first, it is said that God created him in his own image. This speaks to me of form and individuality, uniqueness and personhood, recognizable by what we call *shape*. Then, we are told, God breathed into man his own divine breath—his own spirit—so that man became a living soul. To me, this speaks of those incorporeal elements of our being—mind or reason, emotion or feeling, discrimination or taste, and more important than all, conscience. These characteristics of being reside *within* and constitute the human temperament and its singular power of choice. Together, *shape* and *spirit* make up the human being created *in imago dei,* in the image of God—which means, among other things, that human beings possess physical attributes through which to perform conscious choices, expressions of free will communicated and illumined by reason.

But with these attributes also came obligations belonging exclusively to the creature made in God's image, possessing God's own breath of life. This creature called Man was commissioned to exercise God-given authority over every aspect of nature; he was called to name the animals and to tend the Garden of God. He was ordained to be the responsible creature, caring for animate and inanimate creatures alike: communicating with them and enjoying their discovery of what it means to fly, swim, or walk; appreciating in the stillness of a stone the mystery of its relationship to the Creator.

Closest to him among all other creatures was the Woman who, by her union with her husband, shared his authority in Eden and brought to completion the meaning of what it is to be human. Together Man and Woman delighted in their environment, their joy springing from freedom found in obedience and from purpose found in rewarding work. That work I take to have been the constant offering up to the Creator of new arrangements of flowers and trees, new shapes to ornamental shrubs, new names for strange beasts and birds just discovered in some remote glen, new songs in praise of the Creator whose love for his Creation was reflected daily in Adam and Eve's love for each other. Art is the artist's own expression of love. The purpose of making a work of art is to manifest in concrete form some token of an indissoluble bond between lovers. In time, Adam's love for Eve, and their love for the Creator, would show itself in the reproduction of human life, but humanity's first works of art, we infer from Genesis 2, may have been landscape gardening and poetry, a testament to human pleasure in offering back to God some outpouring of Man's own imagination. All art is sacrifice, giving back from where it came the best of what we have held in trust.

But notice carefully that Adam never possessed God's inimitable power to *create*. When God the Father willed the world into being, when God the Son spoke the world into beauty, when God the Spirit illumined the world with the light of love, the Trinity working in perfect concord caused the cosmos to be formed *ex nihilo*, that is, out of nothing. Only the God who is himself "wholly other," as Rudolph Otto has taught us to say, only the God for whom the act of Creation itself is a series of spontaneous *ooh*'s and *ah*'s of delight in the goodness of it all—only this God could *create*. He is the God of whom the English hymnwriter John Mason has said,

> Thou wast, O Lord, and Thou wast blessed
> Before the world began;
> Of Thine eternity possessed
> Before time's hour-glass ran.
> Thou needest none Thy praise to sing,
> As if Thy joy could fade.
> Could'st Thou have needed anything,
> Thou could'st have nothing made.

God *creates*. He is the Master-Artist, the one whom both the prophet Jeremiah and St. Paul understood as the

Potter. In Jeremiah's vision, as in the apostle's analogy, God is an artist molding the clay as it spins upon his wheel (Jeremiah 18; Romans 9:20-24). His will is sovereign; he forms as he chooses and discards what displeases him, then forms it again. "Surely the potter can do what he likes with the clay" (Romans 9:21), St. Paul declares. I certainly do not claim to know what happened in those transhistorical aeons before the event we call Creation. I merely wonder if this prophetic analogy of the Divine Potter applies beyond Jeremiah's formula for history. Might not the same analogy apply to that description of the cosmos-in-chaos which we find so puzzling in the second sentence of Genesis: "The earth was without form and void"? This statement suggests to me the shapeless mass from which a potter selects a handful of clay and sets it revolving into whatever shape he wishes. But if the clay refuses to be pliable in his hands, if it assumes some shape other than the potter intends, and if he is dissatisfied with his pot, the potter rarely discards the clay. He may smash the flawed and faulty vessel, he may reduce it to broken shards; but he will redeem the clay and use it again to make another pot to his liking. Do not suppose I speak glibly or facetiously when I suggest that Creation, as we struggle to understand it from Scripture, may have been God's fresh energizing of discarded matter. Kneeling over the abyss of darkness, scooping out of the lump of abandoned galaxies the stuff of which we are made, the Father wills the Son to speak and the Spirit to shine. From love to light to life: thus are we formed; and this time the Potter declares that this handiwork is all "very good."

God creates, as St. Basil tells us in the *Hexameron*, "because his name is *Omnipotens Deus,* the Almighty God. . . . His will is action, and he is not weary." Thus the Creator's word of command, "Let there be light," causes light to shine not only on the First Day, but also for as long as the Creator ordains. This fact we celebrate with each day's renewal in words almost too common to carry their real meaning. "Good morning!" is more than merely a greeting; it is an affirmative response to the Creator's own evaluation of his work. Moreover, while it is our privilege as human beings to offer the sacrifice of praise in language, words may not be sufficient in themselves or even necessary; for again to quote St. Basil, "by means of the creatures which he has created in a wondrous manner is his might made known, and he is in this way praised." This means, of course, that simply by each creature's behaving as its creaturely self—whether pebbles, peacocks, or people—the Creator is glorified. A familiar song expresses this fundamental truth:

> Morning has broken like the first morning,
> Blackbird has spoken like the first bird.
> Praise for the singing! Praise for the morning!
> Praise for them, springing fresh from the Word!
>
> Sweet the rain's new fall sunlit from heaven,
> Like the first dew fall on the first grass.
> Praise for the sweetness of the wet garden,
> Sprung in completeness where his feet pass.
>
> Mine is the sunlight! Mine is the morning,
> Born of the one light Eden saw play!
> Praise with elation! Praise every morning,
> God's recreation of the new day.

God creates, Man *imitates*. This is the difference between *poiesis* and *mimesis*, poetry and mimicry, spelled out at greater length in my book, *The Liberating Word: Art and the Mystery of the Gospel*. God wills, and it is done. Yet in his grace, God extends to every human being the same privilege given to Adam and to Eve—the gift of offering back to God daily the best work of our hands. This is God's divine invitation, to "be fruitful and increase, fill the earth and subdue it" (Genesis 1:28). This is God's mandate for us to participate in the fashioning and furbishing of his ongoing Creation.

Under the mandate of Genesis 1 and 2, God the Creator has given human beings all good things to enjoy responsibly. Through common grace, every human being participates in the glory of Creation and is invited to fondle, embrace, and know it as a lover. Because of sin, men still alienated from God usurp to themselves the glory of nature; when they reproduce as art what imagination and reason have perceived, some men dare to call themselves "creative." Redeemed men and women, on the other hand, recognize an obligation to offer their art solely to God as an act of praise and in testimony to their obedience as creatures. A Christian must view his art as one of the Father's gifts. Whatever the artist does—whether he juggles, sings, recites, pirouettes, paints, carves, weaves, cooks, trims, sews, strums, beats, or blows—he does so because God calls him to join in the celebration of all God's wonderful works to the children of men.

We are told that God ceased from all his work and rested on the Seventh Day; but with the dawning of the Eighth Day, the Artist of the Beautiful, the Master Potter, set his Apprentice to work, teaching him to copy the Master's originals, summoning her to image forth new benedictions of praise. If from time to time the Apprentice errs by arrogating to himself credit for alleged creativity, the Master needs only to touch man's puny imitations as a reminder of his utter dependence. For as Eliot again cautions us, in his choruses from "The Rock," there can be no human creativity except that which results from service to God, "which is already His service in creating," writes Eliot. Only as artists committed to sacrifice and service can we be allowed to call ourselves *creative*.

All art is sacrifice, all art is service, and so with Eliot we ask,

> LORD, shall we not bring these gifts to your service?
> Shall we not bring to Your service all our powers
> For life, for dignity, grace and order,
> And intellectual pleasures of the senses?

In attempting to serve God with his art, the artist learns to struggle with words or sounds or paint or stone, none of which he has made. The artist also learns, sooner than later—if he is fortunate and wise—that there can never be more than an illusion of mastery over the medium of his art. The eminent composer Igor Stravinsky, after conducting an almost sublime performance of one of his own compositions, was found offstage in tears of frustration. "It is never good enough!" he lamented.

No, the ecstasies of art, like the ecstasies of love, seem never to be quite enough in and of themselves. Yet no one who has ever known art at its zenith will deny its transcendent power. On a recent Christmas Eve in Cambridge, England, I knelt in King's College Chapel before the altarpiece, Rubens' magnificent "Adoration of the Magi," while the voices of the famous college choir filled the vault with their anthems. Breathtaking architecture, masterly painting, and exultant singing, blending with the spiritual significance of the Eucharist and the Advent season, were almost overwhelming. But I want to be quick to add that to reach that height of near-sublimity, art does not need to be "religious" in any popular sense of the word.

For me, the art of the George Shearing quintet, the chords of the late Duke Ellington's introduction to "Take the A Train," the memory of the late Errol Garner's playing "Misty" for me—or almost any album by the Norman Luboff Choir—these affect me in much the same way. Love, wisdom, and natural beauty come together in richness unmistakable, so that art, in Eliot's words, is recognizable only as "music heard so deeply/ That it is not

heard at all, but you are the music/ While the music lasts."
Yet isn't that precisely the point: "While the music lasts"?
After all, even when one has stood on the summit of
Everest, 29,028 feet above sea level, there is nowhere to go
but down.

So with every human experience, and all the more
since the catastrophe we know as the Fall. Because of disobedience to God, the human race lost that intimate communion with God which marked the Man and Woman's
daily joy; we have lost the full realization of humanity's
special prerogatives as creatures made in God's likeness,
lost the recognition of art as sacrifice and service. We have
entered, instead, upon a dizzying parody of the life God
had intended for his children. Disintegration, alienation,
and death became inexorable consequences of Adam's fall
from grace, our legacy of his disobedience and revolt
against God. As a result of death's ineluctable reality,
nothing in the natural sphere of existence—no single element of living matter, no scintilla of emotion, no filament
of fame—endures beyond its moment in time. The Taj
Mahal, for all the tenderness its beauty evokes, has been
attacked by cruel vandals; the Parthenon, victimized by
the corrosive pollution of modern industry, must now be
sealed from tourists' entering; even the mountains themselves, geologists tell us, are wearing away.

In such a realm ruled by entropy and decay, our culture reflects strivings of human beings to salvage some
moment of tranquility, to preserve some fragment of
peace. The fact of death rages like a fever in the deepest
consciousness of every person. Thus none of these sites of
inestimable beauty can bear the weight of human yearn-
ing for spiritual fulfillment. Aesthetically, emotionally, intellectually, the splendors of nature may appeal, the
edifices of love and piety may arouse, but their effect is
temporary; for over each of them has been written the

dread inscription, "This too shall pass away." So I must backtrack on my journey, from Athens to Jerusalem, not to find some philosophical reply to Tertullian's famous question regarding those two cities, for here philosophy is not our concern. Rather, I am in search of that animating power which alone promises to transform human existence into abundant life, which assures us that "all shall be well, and all manner of thing shall be well."

Come with me, then, not to the Himalayan foothills or to a Mogul emperor's shrine or to an aesthetic wonder. Come with me, instead, along a side street in Jerusalem and through a gate into the confines of a lovely garden. There stand before its rock-face wall, then step into its excavated tomb, prepared for burial. I cannot claim that this is Joseph's garden, but it is a cemetery unlike any other in the world. Here as nowhere else the song of deliverance goes up, "Death is swallowed up; victory is won! O Death, where is your victory? O Death, where is your sting?" (1 Corinthians 15:55). For from such a cave in such a garden stepped forth the Man who had conquered death.

The empty tomb speaks, of course, of that great miracle, the Resurrection. But before there could be a resurrection, there must be an even greater wonder—the Incarnation. As St. Paul told Timothy, "Great indeed, we confess, is the mystery of our religion: 'He was manifested in the flesh' " (1 Timothy 3:16, RSV). From our study of myth and comparative religion, we know that there is nothing exclusively Christian in talking about deity becoming man. Myth and religion throughout the world are full of stories about avatars and apotheosis. What makes the Christian doctrine of the Incarnation unique—not to mention scandalous in certain quarters—is its double claim, that the Incarnation of God in the Person of Jesus of Nazareth is both historical and singular.

God took on human form, Christian doctrine declares,

in the womb of a Jewish virgin living in the province of Galilee in the days when Pontius Pilate was governor, Herod the Great was king, and Augustus was emperor in Rome. *Then and only then.* Christian doctrine does not preclude other theophanies or manifestations of God in human form. Indeed, the Old Testament itself offers several instances, but these are all fleeting appearances. Not until the angelic announcement to Judean shepherds that Christ the Lord had been *born*—not until then, and never again—could one be called *Emmanuel,* "God with us." In that birth Logos and Messiah, the Divine Message and its Messenger, became one: "So the Word became flesh; he came to dwell among us" (John 1:14).

The Incarnation is the key that unlocks God's treasures of wisdom and knowledge. The Incarnation discloses the power to appreciate our senses fully, to perceive something of the transcendent. As William Blake once said,

> To see a world in a grain of sand
> And a heaven in a wild flower,
> Hold infinity in the palm of your hand
> And eternity in an hour.

As Lord of the universe, God-in-Christ absorbs time into his divine being. He comes from before time began in history; he exists beyond the eschaton, the end of time. But in the Person of Jesus of Nazareth, God also occupies a passage of time within history while at the same time he fulfills the mystery described by Malcolm Muggeridge as "now becoming always." Thus the Incarnation becomes "the point of intersection of the timeless with time."

It is not God walking in the Garden in the cool of the day, but God walking

> Where cross the crowded ways of life,
> Where sound the cries of race and clan;
> . . . .
> In haunts of wretchedness and need,
> On shadowed thresholds dark with fears.

The Incarnation is God reasserting, through the promise of redemption, a truth long lost: that, as Paul wrote to Timothy, "everything that God created is good, and nothing is to be rejected when it is taken with thanksgiving, since it is hallowed by God's own word and by prayer" (1 Timothy 4:4, 5).

God's taking on human form in the Person of Jesus of Nazareth remains the paramount act of love in all Creation. In the willingness of God the Father to offer up his only begotten Son, we have the perfect model for selfless giving; for St. Paul has reminded us that God "did not spare his own Son, but gave him up for us all; and with this gift how can he fail to lavish upon us all he has to give?" (Romans 8:32). If art is sacrifice and service, then here—"as an offering and sacrifice whose fragrance is pleasing to God" (Ephesians 5:2)—is God's consummate work of art, just as for human parents the conception and birth of their child is their highest and most godlike attainment. The Incarnation, God's great drama of redemption, is God's way of saying to every human being, "This is who I am; this is what you can be too." Jesus of Nazareth—the one in whom "the complete being of God, by God's own choice, came to dwell" (Colossians 1:19)—is the representation of what Adam was intended to be. Jesus of Nazareth is a work of art in human flesh, reminding us of our destiny.

But more than this: Because Jesus of Nazareth embodies wholly the divine nature of God, he is the perfect blending of matter and spirit. His nature is one, his spirit is in tune with his body. By his very form—by the fleshliness of his flesh, by the rivulets of sweat upon his face, the dust upon his feet; by his hunger, weariness, emotion, passion, death; in short, by his *manhood* Jesus Christ gives sanction and sanctity to all material life, including the human body.

Through the Incarnation, art as sacrifice and art as service become art as sacrament. All of God's Creation is his handiwork; therefore, in each atom, in each molecule, in each facet of nature, animate or inanimate, we may find a visible sign of an inward and invisible grace. Not only in objects, but also in action: eating, working, playing, loving, sleeping are sacraments of the body, in whose shape God chose to become one of us, thereby conferring upon us an everlasting sign of God's pleasure in what he has made.

This sacramental view of nature and human nature converts every natural object and every positive act into a testament to God's grace. Things matter in and of themselves, not just in how we use them. Every piece of bread is a sacrament, every taste of wine, not just those we hallow in the Eucharist. Our recognition of the hierarchies in a beehive or in human social orders intimates our recognition of the cosmic order. No salute, posture, courtesy, or custom—however common or seemingly mundane—is devoid of meaning; it is all part of the courtly dance in celebration of life. As Thomas Howard reminds us in *Chance or the Dance,* "everything means everything."

Consider the handshake. This act carries with it cultural value from the past as well as promise for the future, all signified in the present gesture. Of course it can be trivialized into a commonplace greeting, a sort of mechanical "How are you?" Or it can be transferred into a formality, as at the outset of a wrestling bout. It can even be utilized for character analysis: a handshake strong and grasping or slimy and fishlike. But whatever appears to be a handshake's purpose, it never loses its inherent sacramental value, for a handshake says, "I mean you no harm; I want to be your friend." As a token between wrestling opponents, a handshake says, "I intend to compete with you in fairness and honor. May the best man win."

Germination among plants or procreation among animals is another sacrament confirming God's desire that his creatures should reproduce themselves after their kind. But the act of love between human beings passes beyond mere predictable botanical or biological response to erotic stimuli. In marriage, sexual intercourse becomes a sacred commitment in union between a lover and his beloved. It excludes all other claims and desires. In the act of sexual union, one person says to another, "I offer myself unreservedly to you, holding nothing back; my nakedness is that sign. Take me with all my imperfections of body and soul, and with the perfection of your love, make me to fulfill the ideal I see in you." In sexual intercourse the husband and wife anticipate the act of love alluded to throughout Scripture in metaphors of the Bridegroom and his Bride, the Marriage Supper of the Lamb, the mystery of Christ and his Church. For if these figures of speech have any truth to them at all, what else can a honeymoon signify other than a sacramental foretaste of Heaven? Gnosticism—the denial of the body—is the earliest Christian heresy. Let us not repeat it, for it is in the shape of our human bodies that we are made. As human bodies we live and love; and in these human bodies we come to know God.

This truth receives its highest ratification in the fact of Jesus Christ's resurrection and exaltation. God did not dispense with the crucified body inhabited by Jesus of Nazareth, as though it had then served some temporal and base purpose. Rather, that body has been glorified—although it retains its wounds of suffering and humiliation. That body has been transformed in anticipation of a promise to us: "He will transfigure the body belonging to our humble state, and give it a form like that of his own resplendent body, by the very power which enables him to make all things subject to himself" (Philippians 3:21). And what is that power? Nothing less than the same creative energy that once produced *something* out of *nothing:* the power of his Lordship over the universe, the power of his resurrection.

I often meet people who say, in effect, "What you're talking about is all very nice for the person who considers himself an artist. But I'm no artist. Why, I can't sing a note; I can't even draw a straight line! I work in an office every day filing reports or operating a computer. . . ." The reason such people don't consider themselves artists is not that they have no talent or patience or aren't saintly enough. Rather, the reason is that few of us sufficiently understand the mysteries of Creation, Incarnation, and Vocation; few of us have contemplated these doctrines. Even fewer have responded to the call of God to offer back to him the gifts given to us, thereby raising them above the level of the mundane duty to the sublimity of art itself. Let me try to explain.

In his grace God reaches out to us to help us understand his role and ours as artists in this galactic gallery we call Earth. You and I, by the fact of our re-creation and redemption through the mystery of the Incarnation, are also God's own works of art. This is what Paul writes in his Letter to the Ephesians: "For we are God's handiwork, created in Christ Jesus to devote ourselves to the good deeds for which God has designed us" (Ephesians 2:10). "God's *handiwork*"—the word is *poiema,* the same word from which we have our word *poem* or *poetry.* We are God's poems, written in the same meter and rhythm, the same form and shape, as the Incarnate Word himself. In the orders of Creation, as poems we are to beget poems; as creatures of his handiwork, we are to be fruitful and multiply, imitating our Divine Original. "What is art," asked Paul Claudel, "if not . . . a sort of mimicry of the Word that creates, the Word that is 'poetry,' a repeating of the *Fiat* which brought everything about?"

The French playwright Jean Cocteau wrote in a letter to his friend Jacques Maritain,

> The marvel of it is that [God] concerns Himself with the tiniest detail of one of the atoms whose swarming makes up the matter of this or that object. But if He counts us, if He counts our hairs, He counts also the syllables of our poems. Everything is His, everything is from Him. . . . We are his poets.

What a responsibility! To be those who by our very bodily presence carry with us the spirit of Christ. For let us not try to escape the consequences of the Incarnation. If Christ is in us, then we have become his incarnate representatives, which means—in the language of C. S. Lewis—that "the whole mass of Christians are the physical organism through which Christ acts—that we are His fingers and muscles, the cells of His body."

The Women's Liberation slogan claims that "Adam was a rough draft." Not so. Adam and Eve were both lyric poems of celebration to God; they were vessels fitted for noble purposes. In their disobedience, however, Adam and Eve debased their gifts to the level of doggerel, to cheap and battered rubbish pails. We too are the sons of Adam, the daughters of Eve; our imitation of the Creator has fallen into disgrace. Yet in his mercy God offers to renew us, fulfilling in us the design intended, making us once again partakers in his own splendor, entrusting to us the Good News—although, as St. Paul says, "we are no better than pots of earthenware to contain this treasure" (2 Corinthians 4:7). Nonetheless we are commissioned to make known the gifts of God, because we are his pots to serve and his poems to praise.

CHAPTER 2

Snapshots or Serious Photography?

A favorite *New Yorker* magazine drawing shows a road-side site for viewing some scenic vista. As a tourist approaches the overlook, two signs point him in opposite directions: "Snapshots" or "Serious Photography." This cartoon, it seems to me, rather well sums up the polar division between popular culture and art in this secular age.

Most of us are casual passers-by, too busy to stop for more than a moment in our hurrying from Here to There. Those who pause to observe the scenery seldom care enough to turn what they see into art. They are not serious photographers hoping to *make* pictures; instead, they want merely to *take* a few snapshots and get back on the road. They have no time to bother with finding a clear focus on the scene or establishing their own perspective and angle of vision. They are not at all concerned about shadings of light or balance of composition. They want to click the camera and be on their way.

This desire for the instamatic experience marks one of the differences between popular culture and genuine art. That difference lies in the degree of seriousness and respect with which art is treated. Not humorless gravity or sanctimonious reverence, but seriousness in the sense of commitment to excellence. Furthermore, this distinction between popular culture and art seriously committed to excellence becomes most apparent when, as Harry Blamires urges, we begin to "think Christianly" about the world around us and its claims upon us.

Popular culture is a product of secularism, which denies the existence of God and attributes ultimate authority to man himself. Secularism knows nothing of art as sacrifice or service to God, nothing of art as a sacrament of the Holy. To the secularist, art belongs to mankind. As Lord Byron wrote,

> 'Tis to create, and in creating live
> A being more intense, that we endow
> With form or fancy, gaining as we give
> The life we image, even as I do now.

One scarcely has to be a critic to recognize the gross disparity between a Christian attitude toward art and the attitude prevailing in our secular world. By common definition, art means *commercial value* as measured by inflationary auction sales at Sotheby's or long lines waiting to hear the ravings of punk rock sadists. Art today appeals to consensus, reaching always for the widest audience, which means finding the lowest common denominator; subject always to the whims of the consumers, which means giving the people what they want. As a result, much of today's art has been debased into popular culture.

Because secularism is enslaved by time and the inevitability of death, popular culture is preoccupied with *quantity* rather than *quality*. If, as secularism claims, life is temporal and fading, with no dimension beyond the grave, then the secularist cannot afford to limit his experience by restricting himself to standards of excellence. He has no time to reserve for the criteria given by St. Paul: "All that is true, all that is noble, all that is just and pure, all that is lovable and gracious, whatever is excellent and admirable—fill all your thoughts with these things" (Philippians 4:8). In searching exclusively for quality, he might become too bogged down by aesthetic scruples and miss out on appealing baubles. So, the secularist reasons, he must keep on the alert, looking constantly for something else, something other, something new; perhaps, if he is lucky, he may attach himself from time to time to something of value.

This is why secular existence is governed by passing fads and trends, styles and fashions, based upon popularity achieved through showmanship and "hype." This is why popular culture thrives upon Top Forty charts and best-seller lists. One successful movie like *Jaws* spawns a flurry of sea terrors; one Broadway hit like *Dracula* produces a rash of horror shows; one exhibitionist like Alice Cooper breeds a horde of imitators. As a result, imagination suffocates, talent is stifled by the rush to conform to popular demand. So the rot spreads like an oil slick, coating everything it touches with decay.

Consider the state of music making in our time. Serious musicians—composers and performers alike—have always wrestled to keep their art free from compromise. But their struggle to resist the siren call of popular culture and remain artists is greater now than ever before. Serious musicians are caught up by today's conglomerate structure, whereby multi-national industries own as subsidiaries not only the music publishing firms and recording companies, but also the agencies and impresarios who stock the concert halls. A cellist or pianist or singer, a composer or conductor must learn to take orders from corporate managers. Business is business, but when "the art of music" becomes the *music business,* as it is today, it isn't the bookkeeping methods that suffer. Accountants with power to decide a concert schedule or the contents of a record album now determine the range of music acceptable to popular culture and dictate which performers will become household names.

And what of those serious musicians whose names are not Jean-Pierre Rampal or Maurice André or Neville Marriner? Most serious musicians join the faculty of some school or college, or they at least teach privately, to support themselves. But others make an adjustment to their pride and step further into compromise by composing or arranging or playing for broadcast commercials, for television movies, or for the major motion pictures themselves. Three friends come immediately to mind. A virtuoso percussionist, who has performed as soloist with orchestras in North and South America, Europe and Asia, depends on his ability to turn one deal after another—making films, promoting a resort, hustling a product—between one-night stands with musical lightweights. He has to make his living somehow. Another friend is a string player, formerly with the London Symphony Orchestra. He has been a booking agent for artists and chamber orchestras touring the world, but now his income is largely derived from contracting musicians to play the film scores for James Bond movies. The third friend is a composer and sometime conductor of almost every leading orchestra in the world, including the New York Philharmonic. He now writes rock-'n-roll tunes under three different pseudonyms.

I intend no criticism of these artists for the decisions they have been forced to make. Even artists must eat, and sometimes they must do what is necessary to make a living, even if their art languishes. But I have heard each of them perform the music he was meant to play—a concerto by Darius Milhaud composed especially for the percussionist, a Mozart symphony at Lincoln Center's Avery Fisher Hall, a Sibelius tone poem at the Hollywood Bowl—and nothing can quite compensate them or us for the bad bargain they have made with popular culture.

Meanwhile, other artists seem to have come to comfortable terms with the monopoly of popular culture. According to *Newsweek* magazine, jazz flutist Herbie Mann says, "Don't let your taste get in the way of reaching a broader audience"—which puts the secular attitude toward music right alongside the selling of deodorant. The largest music publishers, like Chappell, send out monthly reports to their composers-under-contract, telling them what Englebert Humperdinck, for instance, is looking for, thus determining what will be hummed and whistled around the globe according to their sense of "the market."

Popular culture is like a landfill project, building upon mounds of garbage while overhead swarm the devouring predators. No wonder, then, that artists themselves speak with contempt for the trash in which they wade. "We're in a period of the McDonald's of music," says singer Melba Moore, "where it's mass-marketed like junk food. I don't know what *good* is anymore." But if the singer doesn't know, certainly the trash merchants of popular culture, posing as purveyors of art, can tell us their understanding of *good*. Agents, producers, music publishers, recording executives, artist-and-repertory experts, concert managers, publicists, and other parasites and feed off popular culture all know the time-tested slogan of hucksterism: "What smells sells!"

One of the most astonishing features of popular culture is its inability to regard its own products with any degree of seriousness or respect. Disdain for itself results in popular culture's cruel voracity, which engorges today's fad or idol and tomorrow spits it out. Except for a few living legends—Frank Sinatra, some of the aging jazz and blues pioneers like Eubie Blake, and a few deceased stars now elevated to popular sainthood, like Marilyn Monroe, Humphrey Bogart, Elvis Presley—almost nothing and no one survives this orgy of consumption. Look, for example, at the way in which dance rhythms come and go.

In a more courtly era, suites of music bore such designations as waltz, minuet, gigue, and bourrée, each movement comprising a different dance. Today's music-for-dance has lost this breadth and must conform instead to the single compulsive beat. Middle-aged diehards may hold onto their 78 rpm Glenn Miller favorites from the "swing" years, while occasional waves of nostalgia may revive a tepid interest in Chubby Checker's 1960's twist. But no ambitious composer hoping for a hit in the heyday of discomania would dare to revert to any of the outdated rhythms of the past. Cha-cha-cha, meringue, bossa nova, the frug, rock, reggae have all fallen away to be replaced by the newest craze—which in its turn will also die. For in this age of built-in obsolescence and no-fault divorce, popular culture discards its artifacts as easily as a disposable diaper is flushed away.

But more has been lost than just variety in dance steps. More important is the collapse of any serious significance to music and dance, known throughout history in Greek drama and Hebrew psalms. The European society for whom Bach, Handel, Haydn, and Mozart composed their dance music understood the sacramental nature of dance. As long ago as 1531, an ancestor of T. S. Eliot, Sir Thomas Elyot, had written in *A Book Called the Governour* this passage, which the poet quotes in "East Coker," the second of his *Four Quartets:*

> The association of man and woman
> In daunsinge, signifying matrimonie—
> A dignified and commodious sacrament.
> Two and two, necessarye coniunction,
> Holding eche other by the hand or the arm
> Whiche betokeneth concorde.

Where is that sacramental understanding today? Even the dancers themselves seem cut off from any symbolic union or "necessarye coniunction." Instead of "holding eche other," today's whirling dervishes gyrate in isolation, preferring individualism and seeming more concerned about competing against each other than expressing "concorde." As music and dance have become increasingly secularized into entertainment, the sacramental nature of dance as a religious expression of joy has been prostituted into can-can kicklines, homosexual fantasies, and dreary ballrooms where transients can pick up a dancing partner for hire.

So it is throughout popular culture. As in the Taj Mahal Pleasure Palace in New York City—a brothel whose advertising promises, "I'll make you a new man!"—any resemblance between the real thing and its secular defilement is purely illusory. In a culture darkened by denial and frustrated because of disbelief in the very hope whose affirmation brings light, temporal and material claims assert themselves like worm-ridden fruit of the Tree of Knowledge. Secular Man's denial of God—his rejection of Creation, Incarnation, and the Vocation of artist committed to excellence—results in a separation of art from the things of the spirit. From such a separation grows a moral crisis pointing to the collapse of human society itself. We find intimations of collapse in the appalling cultural ignorance of the masses, in glamorization of trivia in our schools and colleges, in destruction of tradition and reverence that have long helped to sustain civilization against barbarism. For example, we are slowly becoming aware that sexual license has left us only a few novelties to enjoy: the corrupting of our own children, orgasms by means of enemas, and ultimately intercourse climaxing in death.

Whenever art ceases to be sacrifice, service, and sacrament, it turns inward and becomes obsessed by the ego of the artist. It ceases to be art and becomes self-gratification, the final phase of its demise into a mere plaything of popular culture. We have come to that point of no return in our civilization, and so we find the current crisis in art at fever pitch where art most markedly affects us— that is, in Emil Brunner's terms, at "that center of existence where we are concerned with the whole . . . with man's relation to God and the being of the person."

A story by Edgar Allan Poe, "The Oval Portrait," illustrates well the nature of the present catastrophe. Poe's story tells of "a maiden of rarest beauty" who marries a painter, "passionate, studious, austere, and having already a bride in his Art." When he paints his wife's likeness, he cries out, "This is indeed *Life* itself!" But she is dead. In accordance with the conventions of a gothic tale, as the last stroke of his brush touches the canvas, the spirit of the woman is extracted from her body to imbue the canvas with a semblance of life. But the portrait is a fraud, for it is not the living, loving organism, the "maiden of rarest beauty"; it is only daubings of oil on canvas. Her husband might have given himself wholly in sacramental expressions of love. Instead, the portrait is an extension of the painter's obsessive ego. To create life lies outside his powers, but he is fully capable of robbing life of its precious vitality, presenting in its place the death mask.

Poe's story is a fantasy, but its gothic terror speaks of the derangement art suffers whenever it becomes obsessed by ego, narcissistic, preoccupied with self, and thereby adulterated into popular culture. In Poe's tale, the painter loses all sense of the presence of a human model, ceases to look at her, and draws instead upon the wild madness within him. "Nothing is so poor and melancholy," wrote George Santayana, "as art that is interested in itself and not in its subject." The professing artist whose primary goal is self-expression is an impostor from whom we learn little about life because he distorts life by centering it around himself.

To disguise his egocentricity, the aesthete may concoct

campaigns on behalf of "art for art's sake" and other expressions of the cult of the Beautiful. The rites of this cult exploit self-indulgence and fascination with the artist's own passions. At its most elemental the cult of the Beautiful reduces to the cult of Self, to the worship of gods made in the image of man, the model for which becomes man's worship of himself. Behind this exaltation of human subjectivity lies hidden the destroying power of the seven deadly sins. "Art for art's sake" translates into "food for food's sake," which is gluttony; "possessions for possessions' sake," which is avarice; "sexual pleasure for pleasure's sake, devoid of responsibility," which is lust; and so on. Chief among all these sins is pride: "everything for my sake."

In the religion of man—which is the religion of secularism—the object of worship is no higher than the worshiper himself. A glance at popular culture exposes that folly; thus, it becomes necessary for an inversion of worship to occur: the deliberate degrading of the image of man to make an idealization of deified man appear more deserving of worship. So, if we are to be honest, the recurring paroxysms by supporters of pornography and sadomasochism in books and movies have nothing to do with the Bill of Rights and freedom of expression. They are really assaults claiming superiority of the individual and his right to usurp the center of reality. Such claims originate in a proud human ego which denies dependence upon a Creator, ignores the need for a Redeemer, and has eliminated the possibility of eternal life. According to this view, the creed of Pythagoras, that "man is the measure of all things," governs the universe, and solipsism—the preeminence of self—becomes the only yardstick for morality.

But, of course, none of this is new. Human vanity has always insisted on establishing its own code of behavior, judging what is best on the basis of what brings the most pleasure. Nineteen centuries ago, the aged Apostle John looked over the hedonistic culture of his day, rife with squalid and dehumanizing practices. He remarked on its transient appeal and contrasted the values of popular culture with a Christian criterion:

> Everything the world affords, all that panders to the appetites or entices the eyes, all the glamour of its life, springs not from the Father but from the godless world. And that world is passing away with all its allurements, but he who does God's will stands for evermore (1 John 2:16, 17).

St. John knew well the sophistry of those who denied that Jesus of Nazareth had been God-in-flesh; he understood also the consequences of that denial. He knew that to do God's will means to stand firmly against the secular presumptions that life is meaningless, that virtue is hypocrisy and Truth a lie.

The doctrine of the Incarnation is rooted in historical reality; its denial is a will-o'-the-wisp, a delusion of crushing significance. For it must be clear that if the Incarnation is false, then there is no divine ideal to imitate, no substance worth embodying as art; therefore, nothing of value. Denying the Incarnation is an attack against the sanctity of human life; denying the Incarnation results in despising all things human, especially the body. By extension, denying the Incarnation cheapens any attempt at a serious commitment to preserving objects of supposed worth and treasure. All this is implicit in the worldly dismissal of serious purpose in art and in the secular preference for pandering to carnal appetites in popular culture.

But to do God's will means to find permanence in a world of change and stability in a quagmire of disappearing values. Doing God's will means asserting belief in the fact of Creation by God the Father Almighty and redemption by the Incarnation of Jesus Christ his only Son our Lord. For the Christian believer, in St. John's time as well as our own, the consequences of belief lead to a universe defined by hope in the Life Everlasting through the power of the Resurrection, witnessed by the revelation of the Holy Spirit in Scripture and in the Church. Because the doctrine of the Incarnation is true, human aspiration to make and preserve imitations of God's Creation as art finds its reasonable explanation: Life is a sacred trust given by God, and physical objects have value as representations of spiritual virtues. Thus the Christian treats the making of art as a sanctifying vocation, but will not waste his time nor spoil his talent on anything demeaning to the Creator.

St. John also knew that the certainty of belief in the Incarnation could never be fully realized until one has first recognized and acknowledged who Jesus Christ is. To break through the limits of disbelief, we need an instance of "the timeless moment," a direct encounter with eternal reality. John, son of Zebedee, had been present at such a moment, when a question was put to a group of men at the Roman village of Caesarea Philippi. Jesus of Nazareth had asked them, "Who do you say I am?" (Matthew 16:15). The answer given by Simon Peter identified Jesus forthrightly, then and for all time: "You are the Messiah, the Son of the living God" (Matthew 16:16). In so articulating his declaration of faith, Simon Peter had perceived, beyond any ability of his to explain, the mystery of God's divine vertical intervention into linear history. Here is "the point of intersection of the timeless/ With time."

The Incarnation draws indelibly the sign of the cross with all its scandal and glory. For only by the scandal of the cross may we know or refuse to know the glorious truth of the gospel, that "God was in Christ reconciling the world to himself" (2 Corinthians 5:19). In that act of reconciliation, the Incarnate Lord of the universe himself passed through the refining fires of human suffering and by the glory of his divinity purged death of its dross. He transformed mere existence into abundant life and by his benediction upon all of human experience—birth and death, weddings and funerals—restored meaning and purpose to living.

So the question from Caesarea Philippi and its apostolic reply echo across the centuries. Yet how can it not seem absurd to a secular-minded person today? To a painter on upper Madison Avenue or to a country music singer trying to make it big in Nashville, what could be more irrelevant than to ask him who Jesus Christ is? What has Jesus Christ to do with the Top Forty, the best-seller list? Did he ever make it to Carnegie Hall? But ridiculing the question will not make it go away. Pharisee and publican, centurion and governor, disciple and demoniac alike were all compelled to answer this same inescapable question. In spite of themselves, rock singers and sculptors and concert pianists, gourmet chefs and novelists and jazz trumpeters—as well as all of us who make up their constituency—must come face to face with the issue of Jesus Christ's identity. They must weigh for themselves the relative values between admitting who Jesus is and committing themselves to him or choosing to reject him.

Those who accept the challenge and, like Simon Peter, confess their belief will find that their gifts, long buried in the slime of popular culture, can be redeemed and a renewed purpose found in their calling to serve God as artists. But those who reject Jesus Christ and his claims are in double jeopardy, for not only do they commit an affront to God's well-beloved Son but also a crime against the sanctity of the human imagination. Their rejection of Jesus Christ is the final irrationality. "Art," said Jean Cocteau, "is not a pastime but a priesthood." In so saying, Cocteau defines the sacramental nature of art, its implicit spiritual power. To waste our gifts is self-condemnation, for to make of art anything less than its seriousness merits is worse than folly; it is an unpardonable sin.

The Work of Our Hands

When our children were in elementary school, one of our joyful duties was to receive the daily products of their art class. Like so many other parents, we began taping their colorful scrawls to the refrigerator door, as if they were new acquisitions in the Museum of Modern Art. But as quantity exceeded available space, my wife settled upon a plan: At the end of each week, one representative drawing by each child would be displayed. But which drawing? Obviously, only that week's best work. From an ecstatic and indiscriminate acceptance of any and all sketches, we were now compelling ourselves and our children to make decisions of relative value: "This drawing is better than these."

In time, those kindergarten dabblers have grown to become young adults, leaving behind finger painting and coloring books. In their growing up, they also abandoned John Thompson's "Swans on the Lake" for a Mozart "Fantasia in D minor." Silly Putty gave way to glazed pottery. The role of the Cowardly Lion in a grade-school play was exchanged for Professor Harold Hill in *The Music Man* or Willy Loman in *Death of a Salesman*.

Growth is one of the encouraging signs of the maturing process. Parents watch eagerly for evidence of physical development in height and weight and take serious account of any signs of abnormality. But whereas physical growth has its natural limitations, emotional, intellectual, and spiritual growth should be ongoing. As Christians, we are expected to strive for "mature manhood, measured by nothing less than the full stature of Christ," says St. Paul.

> We are no longer to be children, tossed by the waves and whirled about by every fresh gust of teaching, dupes of crafty rogues and their deceitful schemes. No, let us speak the truth in love; so shall we fully grow up into Christ. He is the head, and on him the whole body depends. Bonded and knit together by every constituent joint, the whole frame grows through the due activity of each part, and builds itself up in love (Ephesians 4:14-16).

As we mature physically and spiritually, we must also mature emotionally and intellectually in our response to others, in our reactions to the culture that seeks to overwhelm us. One of the checkpoints of maturity ought to be a growing discrimination in art. We rightly expect someone, after reasonable instruction and experience, to acquire mature tastes—to be able to discern differences between the genuine and the specious, the brilliant and gaudy, the appropriate and tasteless; to differentiate integrity from fragmentation, sensibility from sentimentality; to distinguish between the authentic and the merely cute. In every person's progress toward emotional and intellectual maturity, a point must be reached when an eye-catching bauble is examined more closely to see why it appeals, to ask if its appeal stems from natural integral beauty or from some external emotion brought to the object by the one who fondles it. It may be pretty, it may carry with it pleasing associations—but is it *art*?

For example, to mature musically is to recognize differences between, say, Handel's *Royal Fireworks Music* and the sham pyrotechnics in a film score of a Hollywood spectacular. Or to appreciate the fusion of music and lyrics in a Stevie Wonder song such as "You Are the Sunshine of My Life," as against the mindlessness of the Doobie Brothers singing "Jesus Is Just Alright with Me." To mature as a viewer of paintings is to look beyond representational figures for lines of power and concentration, for chiaroscuro effects, for selectivity of materials. A mature reader welcomes the narrative of inner drama—the kind of story that bores the immature because nothing appears to be happening. A response to structural integrity; a surge of joy at the quiet dynamism of understatement; an immediate recoil from anything—any device of rhetoric, any splash of paint—that seeks to draw attention to itself at the expense of the whole work: These are a few criteria for the mature appreciation of art.

In plain terms, maturity presupposes that our response to art will pass beyond an adolescent "I like it" or "I don't like it." For Christians particularly, there must be a higher standard of appreciation and judgment, but finding that standard does not mean identifying and then labeling certain works as "Christian." Within the Church, and especially within its evangelical subculture, we hear a great deal about "Christian education" by "Christian teachers" or "Christian television and radio" programmed by "Christian broadcasters." We have "Christian psychology," "Christian cosmetics," even "Christian Yellow Pages." It's natural, I suppose, in such a climate to speak of "Christian art" produced by "Christian artists" and of "Christian books" written by "Christian authors," sold by "Christian booksellers." But what do these designations mean? Are they valid? By what objective standards may a confessing Christian's work be judged to be "Christian"?

To answer such questions requires spiritual maturity, demonstrated by an understanding that genuine art knows no distinction between "sacred" and "nonsacred." Played to the glory of God, a wordless Bach fugue is equally as sacred as the chorale "O Sacred Head Sore Wounded"—whose melodic origins, interestingly enough, are as a drinking song. Often, because a work of art, such as a Bach fugue or a Renoir portrait, requires great seriousness of concentration to appreciate its balanced simplicity and complexity, the allegedly nonsacred work speaks more profoundly than does the music or painting we experience Sunday after Sunday in our churches. Art, to be art, must be true; the source of all truth is God; therefore, art needs no special designations to justify itself.

When both the artist and his audience enter wholly into a full appreciation of God's work in Creation and mankind's role as his imitators, then Christians will be able to dissolve the capricious and arbitrary division between "sacred" and "nonsacred" art. Christians will be able to accept with confidence the assurance that all of Creation exists "to be enjoyed with thanksgiving by believers who have inward knowledge of the truth" (1 Timothy 4:3). Sadly, however, what we all too often find in the Church is immaturity among Christians, like those in Corinth, whom St. Paul rebuked "as infants in Christ." Their spiritual immaturity had made them ineligible for the strong meat they should have been able to assimilate, "and so," Paul told them, "I gave you milk to drink, instead of solid food, for which you were not yet ready" (1 Corinthians 3:1, 2).

Throughout the Church the infant's diet still prevails, especially when it comes to considering how art can be put to service for Jesus Christ. Because of spiritual immaturity, a frothy effervescence masquerades as joy; cant phrases bludgeoned into meaninglessness presume to express belief. The absence of serious thought or intelligent concern for appropriateness, decorum, or taste shows how little we care about what it means to possess "the mind of Christ" (1

Corinthians 2:16). As a result, a schism divides biblical standards for truth and excellence from what the Church commonly accepts as art. While we claim to know the creative and redeeming power of God, spiritually immature attitudes toward art reveal that the consequences of the Fall still affect the aesthetics of our lives. We have been taken over by what David Poling calls "the spiritual-babes-in-joyland approach" which promotes "an anemic, pablum-coated gospel that passes for the real thing." He is right. Through tasteless and wrongheaded leadership, most of what passes for art in our churches, schools, and colleges, in our broadcasting media, in our films and literature never belonged there in the first place.

Ugly and *irrelevant, superficial* and *tawdry, garish* and *meretricious:* These are strong words, I know, but they accurately describe much of the alleged art offered in the name of Christ. Portraits of Jesus romanticized into Anglo-Saxon chauvinism; gospel musicians in clown costume and singing vaudeville songs; poetry so overripe in sentimentality, its bathos causes tears of comic relief. When Eliot himself looked at the quality of "religious verse," and was asked why so little of it reaches a high standard, he answered, "Largely, I think, because of a pious insincerity," and then he explained:

> The capacity for writing poetry is rare; the capacity for religious emotion of the first intensity is rare, and it is to be expected that the existence of both capacities in the same individual should be rarer still. People who write devotional verse are usually writing as they *want* to feel, rather than as they do feel.

Furthermore, instead of bringing our gift for making art, along with everything else in our lives, into subjection to the Lordship of Jesus Christ, we go on looking at God's Creation with eyes myopic or half-focused; we hear through clogged ears; we taste, but our palates are still tainted by an aftertaste of the old wine.

Let me be utterly blunt. We live in a cultural wasteland populated—if not governed—by Yahoos, some of the worst of whom may well be evangelical Yahoos. One of the most discouraging aspects of my frequent visits to college campuses, particularly to evangelical Christian colleges, is the apparent failure on the part of many administrators, chaplains, and deans of student affairs to perceive the correlation between spiritual maturity and aesthetic discrimination. This failure shows itself most prominently in the use of funds by student committees to sponsor concerts and other "cultural events." Here we have a supposedly academic community—a group of select young people and their Christian mentors—with a budget to spend. How do they choose to spend that money? More often than not on the kind of entertainment spilled over from popular culture's offscourings—the secular world's trash doctored up to seem "Christian" by its lyrics adapted from Bible verses and its charismatic clichés.

Bring to the campus a genuine artist—a singer who doesn't need a ridiculous array of electronic equipment to project his pipsqueak voice, an actress who can change even a lecture hall into a world of her own imagining, a poet whose language carries his audience away, a choir or orchestra whose music rings with richness and authenticity—and ticket sales may not meet the minimum required by the college comptroller. But advertise the latest imitators of the pop scene—a "born again" version of KISS or The Beach Boys—and the dormitories are emptied, with resident counselors and assistant deans (taking time off from their graduate studies in Higher Education, no doubt) in the front rows. Have they not read these words?

For indeed, though by this time you ought to be teachers, you need someone to teach you the ABC of God's oracles over again; it has come to this, that you need milk instead of solid food. Anyone who lives on milk, being an infant, does not know what is right. But grown men can take solid food; their perceptions are trained by long use to discriminate between good and evil (Hebrews 5:12-14).

You think I am being too harsh? Then I invite you to join me for a few minutes of browsing in almost any bookstore catering to the evangelical trade; or, if you prefer, leaf through current issues of evangelical periodicals, studying the advertising. Much of the evidence, I'm afraid, testifies to a clientele eager for the sentimental or the sensational, with an abundance of producers willing to supply their demand. In many respects, evangelical preference appears to be no different from secular appetites, appealing as always to the lust of the flesh, the lust of the eyes, and the pride of life.

In fairness, the Christian who owns a bookstore cannot be held solely to blame for the sterile quality of the products displayed and sold. Shopkeepers, one may argue, are only agents operating between manufacturers and consumers. We don't necessarily blame the local supermarket manager for the fact that ITT's Wonder Bread tastes like straw. But, of course, if it's a better quality of bread we want, we can usually find an authentic bakery nearby whose whole grain bread provides a nourishing alternative to the tasteless product. The same is not always the case when we are shopping for a missionary biography or Easter anthem, supplies for Vacation Bible School or a sympathy card whose consolation expresses a Christian attitude toward death. The average bookstore or gift shop in our suburban malls simply ignores the evangelical customer's need for a specialized merchandise; so we are left with no choice but to patronize the nearest Christian bookstore we can locate.

In the typical Christian bookstore, you expect to find Bibles and commentaries, books of inspiration, instruction, and devotion, sheet music and recordings of gospel songs, and education aids for the church. But what is overwhelming is the inventory of mobiles, posters, plaques, decals, greeting cards, buttons, lapel pins, candles, bookends, key rings, wallets, belts, games, needlepoint and macrame sets, place mats, napkins, glasses, calendars, pens and pencils. Anything you can buy in the local 5-and-10 cent store is also for sale at Mary and Martha's or The Emmaus Inn. (By the way, today's stores have long since ceased to be known by such low-key names as Bible Book Nook.) Of course, these bric-a-brac are different from what you find at Woolworth's or K-Mart in one obvious way. Embossed, engraved, inscribed, or otherwise imprinted on every object is a token that presumably makes the item "Christian." The most common sign is a cross, but the phrase "Praise the Lord" will serve the same purpose, turning knickknacks into "Christian art." But what is particularly "Christian" about any of these articles for sale—this leather handbag or that woodcarving spelling "MOM," or that baseball cap, whose advertisment reads, "Full line of Religious Glitter"? The problem seems to be that what is packaged and delivered to us by these manufacturers lacks authenticity. Its Christianity is superficial, pasted on the outside. But once the decal has peeled off, one coffee mug looks pretty much like all the rest. What makes it "Christian" then?

A conversation with a potter comes to mind. He had asked: If it were possible to make a "Christian pitcher," what would it look like? How would it differ from any other vessel used to pour beverages? We agreed from the outset that no such container existed, but for the sake of discussion we could make these hypothetical suggestions. First, such a piece of pottery holds whatever liquid it contains without leaking. This pitcher stands firmly on its base without tipping over. It may be of almost any shape imaginable, so long as it fulfills its intended purpose to serve as a pitcher. It is what it is, without apology or explanation. Therefore, it needs no emblems to mark it as "Christian." In fact, anything external to its grace as an object and its function as a utensil is mere advertising or propaganda, not art. We also agreed that it is unthinkable to consider praising the Lord, no matter how boldly the message is inscribed, with a flawed or faulty pitcher.

The late W. H. Auden called much of what he saw in the guise of Christian art "vast quantities of phony or vulgar trash." Auden went on to say, "When one looks into the window of a store which sells devotional art objects, one can't help wishing the iconoclasts had won." John Lawing observes that "gospel garbage is a big money maker." Reporting on the national convention of the Christian Booksellers Association, Lawing sees that "God and mammon are not as far apart as some suppose." It was not always so. For decades the bookstore specializing in books and other products for Christians barely survived on the sale of prizes for the Sunday School picnic and Bibles for special occasions. But how things have changed in America! A recent Gallup Poll claims that one-third of the population identifies with "born-again Christians"; almost 40 per cent of the college freshmen in the fall of 1978 acknowledged a religious experience in their lives which they called "being born again." With this sudden surfacing of a Christian sector in the population have come thousands of new ideas to reap a financial harvest from fresh territory and sales to astonish even the most skeptical marketing director.

Success also brings problems, which John T. Bass, executive vice-president of Christian Booksellers Association, rightly describes as resulting from an imbalance between the ministry of the Christian merchant and his concerns as a businessman. Bass calls for a renewed commitment to maintaining this balance, citing the 1979 CBA convention's watchword, "Making Christ Known," as an instrument "to carry awesome motivational support as a theme for booksellers and suppliers to rally behind during the eighties." Bass has the right perspective on this matter. No reasonable person—least of all a writer dependent on sales of his books for royalties!—begrudges a profit to the Christian who publishes or sells those books or operates any legitimate business or profession. The economics of Scripture clearly declares that "the worker earns his pay" (Luke 10:7; 1 Timothy 5:18). But that same worker has an obligation, whatever that work may be, both to God and to those who pay for his services. If he regards his work as a vocation for God, he must follow the instructions given by St. Paul to the Ephesians—"as God has called you, live up to your calling" (Ephesians 4:1)—and to Timothy:

> Try hard to show yourself worthy of God's approval, as a labourer who need not be ashamed; be straightforward in your proclamation of the truth (2 Timothy 2:15).

Only a few minutes on the showroom floor at the Christian Booksellers convention, or a glance through the CBA house organ, *Bookstore Journal,* leads one to wonder if all those laborers in the business of manufacturing and marketing products with Christian labels have the same noble purpose. Frankly, it seems more like passing through the suburbs of Vanity Fair. If some of the advertising is abominable, the products themselves can only be worse. Here, look and judge for yourself. Notice the mediocrity and sheer cheapness of so much being offered! And beyond the stench of cheapness, the blatant attempt of entrepreneurs to capitalize on the latest spiritual fad is a noxious reminder of popular culture at its worst.

T-shirts are hot sellers, and one manufacturer exhibits the latest fashion: from Warner Brothers comes permission to use cartoon characters preaching catchy sermons. The

Roadrunner is "Joggin' for Jesus! Beep-Beep!" Tweety Bird says, "Big or Small, God Wuvs Us All." The Bandito holds his dueling pistols in a threatening pose and warns, "Heaven or Hell? Turn or Burn," while Porky Pig lifts his cap in a farewell salute that reads, "Armageddon. That's all, folks." And for the benefit of 1979 television fans, this purveyor of sanctified underwear offers Mork's hand signal and the message, "Na-no Na-no. God Loves You."

The next booth displays "Christian jewelry" shaped to form a word or sign: JESUS or the Greek letters Alpha and Omega, a fish or a dove. Rings, earrings, tie clasps, stick pins, belt buckles, necklaces, bracelets—but what makes them "Christian"? One can scarcely point to the craftsmanship, which can be equaled or surpassed in almost any mail order catalogue. Yet even when the workmanship bears the Tiffany hallmark, if you take away the words "TRY JESUS," can the lapel pin still be called "Christian jewelry"? Is there some mystical quality, some anagogic representation, inherent in the signs and symbols familiar to Christians? If so, then what transforms a cross, burning on the lawn of a black family, into a symbol of hatred? When is a fish a visual acronym for *Jesus Christ, God's Son, Savior,* and when is it a logotype for a seafood restaurant? When is a bird a sign of the dove, and not merely a pigeon?

Have you noticed the tendency of advertisements to be extravagant, even to the point of silliness? Over here, among the reproductions of paintings, offered as greeting cards, note paper, and lithographed prints for framing, is an unfortunate example. It's a set reconstructing scenes from the Bible, like a slide-show from the Holy Land underscored by the strains of "I Walked Today Where Jesus Walked." The figures are sentimental, some of the locations are historically disputable. All in all, the work is hardly in a class with the masters—say, Rembrandt's "Return of the Prodigal Son" or Honthorst's "Christ Before the

High Priest." Perhaps the artist himself is a little embarrassed by promotion of his work that claims, "This inspiring collection will add a new dimension to Christian art."

But wait! Here's just the thing: "America's Calendar Beautiful" featuring "lovely full-color photography of God's majesty in nature with fitting verses from Scripture." That certainly seems authentic enough, and the nice part is the packaging by the manufacturer—"DISPLAY PACK FOR IMPULSE PURCHASE." The idea is simple: The proprietor of a Christian store places the box of calendars near his cash register and slowly returns the customer's change by passing his hand over the calendars. Or better yet, you can have your name imprinted on the calendars and *give them away*! "A tasteful and thoughtful good-will builder that reflects well on you—and keeps your name prominent all year long."

Had enough of our tour of trinkets and doodads? We can't stop here, however, because the best is yet to come—the music industry and its sideshows. Here's where the real promotional dollar is spent, with personal appearances by competing singing groups to sell their recordings and sheet music. Each singer comes more highly touted than the other, and superlatives gush in abundance.

America's number one premier vocal group!

You've SEEN her on "Name That Tune" and "Hee Haw Honeys." Now HEAR her on . . .

A fresh statement of faith by one of America's brightest new talents.

Enjoy the exciting music talents of the top names in the Christian music field.

The ultimate in vocal sound and ministry.

This hyperbole is breathtaking, even for a commercial venture so sensitive to the pulse rate of *Variety* and *Billboard* opinion makers as is "the Christian music field." But what else can you expect? The business of publishing and recording music sung by and for Christians takes its cue, not from the saints which are in Waco, Texas, but from secular-motivated artist-and-repertory experts in Hollywood, Nashville, and New York.

Four executives in the recording industry give their views on the direction their ministry is taking. Billy Ray Hearn, president of Sparrow Records, says, "Contemporary Christian music will go where the pop music goes. The culture dictates what pop music does." Hearn justifies "keeping in touch with the world's sounds" on the grounds that "you don't play Chinese music in Africa to convert them, and to the person on the street you don't play 1950 rock and roll." While Bob MacKenzie, president of NewPak Records and Paragon Music, argues for producing music that will "have a bite to it and challenge the mores of the times," he also confirms his intentions to follow somebody else's lead: "For the future, we will go where the music goes, as many directions as there are listeners to hear. We will be in tune with the beat and spirit of the times." Another spokesman, Greg Nelson of Spirit Records, declares, "I'm going to stick with where the kids are at and with what works." A fourth, Bill Cole, vice-president of Light Records, concedes that "secular or pop music is already established with Christian young people. One of the challenges we face is to broaden the base of musical interest of contemporary Christian music and have Christian music become part of this life."

How these business strategies square with St. Paul's command, "Adapt yourselves no longer to the pattern of this present world" (Romans 12:2), is not for anyone else to judge. But on the surface, at least, there appears to be a contradiction between the A-and-R men and the apostle.

Or maybe it's just that Paul didn't understand the music business and never had to face the bottom line! The choice seems to be between adhering to "the beat and spirit of the times" and sticking with "where the kids are at" or obeying Scripture, which in J. B. Phillips' version says, "Don't let the world around you squeeze you into its mould." From the wizards at Columbia, ABC Records, Atlantic, Motown, or Warner Brothers—who make their fortunes by predicting the next wrinkle in popular taste—the advice is simple: Get with it! Go with disco, go with rhythm-and-blues, go with country, go with middle-of-the-road. Go with whatever will get you there! Make up the words as you go along, but keep the beat strong. That's what sells records today. But following this advice imperils what John Bass calls "the balanced role of ministry and business."

Nonetheless the compromises are forged: Make the music sound like what the world most wants to hear at the moment, but use words that will transform the song into a gospel witness. Unfortunately, as any artist knows, art seldom works that way. The problem for the Christian artist converges on both spiritual and intellectual immaturity. On the spiritual front, commercial necessity is at war with the priorities of Christian vocation, a conflict which can only be resolved where the Cross and the Empty Tomb intersect with the life of the musician. On the intellectual side, the problem is an underdeveloped understanding that form and content together determine the effect of a song. Art consists in the bringing together of many elements in a single composition, in an integral relationship of parts-to-whole. In song writing, a careful lyricist chooses not only his words, but his vowels and consonants and syllables to fit the melody line or meter. Once a poem has been set to music, or once music has been grafted into language, there is no "message" in the music or lyrics alone.

To make the point dramatically, try adapting Donna Summer's disco orgy by changing the words from "Love to Love You Baby" to "Love to Love You Jesus." But if that thought offends you—although the suggestion is hardly any more sacrilegious than the surreality of gospel songs such as "Drop Kick Me, Jesus, Through the Goal Posts of Life" or "He's More Than Just a Swearword"—if you find that transposition too repulsive, consider something more tame. Sing "The Lord's my Shepherd, I'll not want," not to the tune "Crimond" or "Wiltshire," but to the rousing United States Marine Hymn:

> From the halls of Montezuma
> To the shores of Tripoli . . .

See how well the words fit the meter? So what difference does it make? What difference indeed! To take the Psalter paraphrase of Psalm 23 and rob its pastoral language from blending with an appropriate melody, harmony, rhythm, and meter is a musical outrage. Even the most tone-deaf disco deejay knows the importance of form in expressing content. Why, then, should it be so difficult for evangelical Christians to comprehend? Beyond music, why do we continue to measure such a profound incongruity between our professed love for God and the quality of art produced by Christians and supported by Christians?

Perhaps the reason for this appalling disparity between evangelical fervor and much of our supposed art resides in our spiritual and aesthetic immaturity. We have not yet grown up in Christ. We have not learned the meaning of the doctrine of Vocation, the significance of the work of our hands in the Kingdom of God. We seem not to know that God's calling Adam in Eden has its parallel in the call given by Jesus of Nazareth. He calls Simon of Capernaum and Nathanael of Bethsaida and Mary of Magdala and Saul of Tarsus; he also calls you and me. We are called to learn from him as apprentice artists in the Master's studio, working and working until what we have made brings glory rather than shame to the Master Artist whose name is to be stamped on our work. We are called to serve him, but not as employees or time-pleasers, because the work to which we are called, as Eliot reminds us, is

> No occupation either, but something given
> And taken, in a lifetime's death in love,
> Ardour and selflessness and self-surrender.

This is the meaning of sacrifice and service, marked, as Eliot says, by "prayer, observance, discipline, thought, and action." These are all sacraments of a vocation realized and fulfilled only through patience and hard work. The gospel of Jesus Christ and the vocation to which he calls us offer no easy options. There is no place for highbrow snobbery or lowbrow vulgarity; for as Jean Cocteau perceived, the mature Christian knows an alternative to either aesthetic elitism—art exclusively for the connoisseur—or popular culture—giving the masses what they want. "Art for art's sake, or for the people, are equally absurd," Cocteau wrote to Jacques Maritain. "I propose art for God."

How does "art for God" differ from "Christian art"? An artist knows that the word *Christian* is primarily a noun, not an adjective. The word *Christian* denotes a substantive fact, not a subjective judgment. Any expression of faith in Jesus Christ resides in the one who makes a work of art and in those who find within it a means of grace and an avenue for praise. Not in the song, but in the singer and listeners; not in the paint, but in the painter and viewers. The fact that the artist believes is this: Jesus Christ has redeemed not only his soul, but all of Creation; not only his heart and mind, but also his gifts for seeing, feeling, hearing—all his physical senses. Thereafter, the Lord of the universe calls him to offer back in return the products of those senses. Given back to God as expressions of love and praise, these works of art need no *imprimatur*, no sloganeering to make them "Christian." No verse of Scripture tacked onto a painting or poster transforms the picture into anything "Christian," especially if it is not of excellent quality to begin with.

If ever a writer professing to be a Christian qualified as a "Christian writer," the late C. S. Lewis would have deserved that nomination. But, as we have already said, there is no specifically "Christian art," no special category of authors writing "Christian books." "Christian literature," says Lewis, "can exist only in the same sense in which Christian cookery might exist." And then Lewis shows the absurdity of these distinctions by adding, "Boiling an egg is the same process whether you are a Christian or a Pagan." Similarly, the poet W. H. Auden declares, "There can no more be a 'Christian' art than there can be a Christian science or a Christian diet."

A friend of mine once asked a waitress for a "Jewish pickle" to go with her cheeseburger. The waitress replied, "Our pickles don't have any religion." Both Lewis and Auden would have agreed with the waitress. At the risk of appearing overly obvious, it seems well to point out that pickles and books and most other objects for sale are in themselves neutral, without spiritual weight or dimension: they have no religion. To be sure, some pickles are different from others, which is why the H. J. Heinz Company has been able to thrive on its 57 varieties. Presumably both the kosher pickle and the evangelical best seller differ from their respective counterparts in being ritually "clean." Furthermore, the pickle jar bears a label denoting its rabbinical authorization; the evangelical best seller almost certainly carries a Foreword written by a household name and corresponding to a Roman Catholic cardinal's *nihil obstat*. But no pickle and no book is holy of itself; it possesses no saving virtue. The fact is that there is no visible difference between books written by Christians and those written by disbelievers. They don't have to be published in Grand Rapids or Wheaton; they don't have to deal with life in the parsonage or recount some romanticized version of a Bible story. But inherently the work of a writer who is a Christian will be different from the disbeliever's, and that difference will show itself in attitudes appropriate to biblical principles. As Auden says, "There can only be a Christian spirit in which an artist . . . works or does not work."

That spirit of which Auden speaks is given by God the Spirit of truth, promised by Jesus Christ himself. Imbued by this divine spirit through faith in Christ, the artist expresses a desire for integrity and excellence in his work, seasoned with humility. The artist is freed from bondage to his own ego and its need to center all credit for creativity and praise for inspired genius upon himself. He knows that he is not the originator, only the channel through whom the work of art becomes visible. Once conscious of his privileged role as God's apprentice, the artist labors to make his work wholly consistent with his creed; his art and his faith become one expression. The artist's aim is to make art worthy of his calling and to present that art in worship to God. His art must strive for nothing less than excellence, for in the worship of God man is challenged by the presence of none other than the Creator himself. Man's gift in worship can never match the glory of God; yet we are invited to offer all we are and have in tribute to the One in whose image we are created.

We should not hesitate to strive for excellence because of fear that our gifts may be less than another's. Harold M. Best speaks to this point when he writes,

> What is excellence, anyway? . . . It is both absolute and relative; absolute, because it is the norm of stewardship and cannot be avoided or compromised; relative, because it is set in the context of striving, wrestling, hungering, thirsting,

pressing on from point to point and achievement to achievement.

"Moreover," Best continues, "we are unequally gifted and cannot equally achieve. Consequently, some artists are better than others. But all artists can be better than they once were. This is excelling."

Art for God leaves no place for cheap or base workmanship. Nothing tarnished or tainted belongs to the vocation of the artist called by Jesus Christ. Motives may be honorable—the salvation of souls, the unity of the Body of Christ—but good intentions are not enough. Elton Trueblood warns us, "Holy shoddy is still shoddy." In *The Book of Common Prayer*, Miles Coverdale's translation of Psalm 90 ends with these soaring words:

> Show thy servants thy work, and their children thy glory. And the glorious majesty of the Lord our God be upon us: prosper thou the work of our hands upon us; O prosper thou our handy-work (Psalm 90:16, 17).

Once we have seen the work of God's Creation, we cannot pray for the grace of divine benediction to be upon anything less than our best. For on a Day yet to come, each of us will be summoned to present an accounting of what we have done with the talents given to us. Jesus' parables concerning stewardship and Paul's analogies to the master-builder and the athlete in the Games all point to the same truth: God demands the best and rewards accordingly. To be an artist is a vocation requiring the kind of effort worthy of the Olympic laurel wreath. The artist who is a Christian can set no goal less than this, "to win the prize which is God's call to the life above, in Christ Jesus" (Philippians 3:14).

Furthermore, on that Day we shall be called to share in decorating the New Jerusalem. This ultimate invitation from God the Father to each of his children commands us to bring before him the work of our hands. What will that work be? Plastic and tinsel and glitter and veneer? Clichés and hype and press releases and slogans? Or will we be able to present our portion of what the Apostle John sees as "the wealth and splendour of the nations" (Revelation 21:26)? The work of our hands ought to be "art for God."

C H A P T E R 4

Art and the Things of the Spirit

One of my favorite stories in the Old Testament is an ob-
scure moment in the life of David; yet it is a moment
significant enough to be recorded twice in Scripture. David
is being pursued by Saul, while at the same time the Philistines are occupying part of Saul's kingdom, including
Bethlehem. David grows homesick and weary of the fugi-
tive's life, and in an outburst of anguish he exclaims, "If
only I could have a drink of water from the well by the
gate of Bethlehem!" (2 Samuel 23:15). Whereupon his
three staunchest heroes—Ishbosheth, Eleazar, and
Shammah—decide to risk their lives to please their leader.
Together they steal through the Philistine lines to
Bethlehem's well and draw a bucket to satisfy David's
thirst. But when they return to the cave of Adullam, David
does a strange thing: He not only refuses to drink the water, but he also pours it out on the ground!

I used to be terribly puzzled by David's act. How un-
grateful, I thought, how capricious, to change his mind so
readily! How thoughtless of the risk his friends had endured on his behalf! But that was before I understood the
meaning of the word *libation*. You see, I had an improper
picture in my mind of David standing outside a cave

dumping a bucket of water like a swill pail. Nothing could be more inaccurate. David wasn't dumping anything; he was offering a sacrifice to the Lord. He wasn't cavalierly emptying a bucket; he was pouring out a libation in thanksgiving to God.

When David looked into that bucket, he saw not the water from Bethlehem's well; he saw instead a gift of love and devotion obtained especially for him at a cost that risked the lives of those who gave it. That bucket of water was, in reality, a bucket of blood—a donation freely offered by three men whose service was a willing sacrifice of themselves in order to procure a sacrament in David's life. In these terms, their gift to him was a work of art—the art of loyal soldiers. In turn, David displays the product of their art, not as self-indulgence but as evidence of his joy in having such faithful friends.

But why not drink it? Why *waste* the water so dangerously obtained? Again, a misuse of language, for the water poured out to the Lord was not *wasted*. It was offered as sacrifice, service, and sacrament, offered in dedication to God. All art, we have said, is sacrifice, service, and sacrament. The very nature of sacrifice calls for a giving away of something of value; service requires the giving away of one's energies; sacrament means giving up an object's apparent usefulness for its real purpose, to represent its higher reality.

This certainly was true of the lamb or young bull presented for burnt offering to the Lord. Once slaughtered and incinerated, any potential commercial value from wool or ox-power had been lost. But in that loss how much more had been gained! So, too, it might be said of our poor offerings. They may represent the fine arts we admire in galleries or in concert halls; they may be the useful arts of hospitality and human concern. No matter, for once the commitment is made, the pledge paid, and our time expended, its worth has been poured out. We have sacrificed the work of our hands.

This is only as it should be. We can never hope to please God by presenting what has been of no cost to ourselves. God demands our best in worship, our best in sacrifice. I do not know what motivated Abel to choose to become a shepherd when his brother Cain chose farming. I am sure there is nothing inherently more pleasing to God about being a shepherd than being a farmer. But Genesis 4 makes it clear that God was pleased by one man's gift and displeased by the other's. Can we understand why? Perhaps one suggestion may be that whereas Abel's lambs were the prizes of his flock, Cain brought bruised and spoiling fruit, the early droppings easily gathered and conveniently offered.

God refuses to settle for second best. Not only is God himself the Master Artist, but he also bestows upon each of us his gifts, asking only that we refine these gifts in order to return to him the works of our hands fit for his praise. The Bible is careful to mention by name various artists who serve as our examples. To Jubal, God gives the gift of playing the harp and flute; to his half-brother Tubal-cain, the gift of metalwork. To Bezalel and Aholiab, he gives his divine spirit making them "skilful and ingenious" in constructing the ornaments of the Tabernacle in the wilderness. To David, he gives the gift of song; to Solomon, wisdom in uttering proverbs; to Hiram of Naphtali, the skill of working in bronze for the Temple on Mount Zion; to the family of Asaph, the art of making music unto the Lord; to Nehemiah, the skill to administer an urban renewal project; to Isaiah, Jeremiah, Ezekiel, and Daniel, the art of foretelling God's plan for his people; to Erastus, the skill of an imperial politician; to Paul, the art of persuasive rhetoric in oratory and letters.

It should be apparent from this roster of biblical personages to whom God entrusted specific gifts that art is not exclusive. There is nothing more sanctifying in writing a song or singing it, whether in Jerusalem's Temple or in the First Baptist Church, than in writing a letter to a friend. Both are opportunities to display the grace of God to others. Nor is art redemptive in and of itself. We are not saved by our art, but by the redeeming death and conquering resurrection of Jesus Christ. Art is one of God's gifts of grace to us in the world, just as Jesus of Nazareth was in the world. This is the sense in which we can say that art, which comes from God, is at the same time made a part of everyday life. Art has been taken out of *sanctum sanctorum*, the Holy of Holies, by the tearing of the veil that separates us from the *shekinah* of God. And what is that torn curtain? Nothing less than the torn and bleeding flesh of God himself in the Person of Jesus of Nazareth.

Yet while art may not be holy of itself and possesses no saving virtues, nonetheless art remains one of God's great gifts of common grace. Therefore, I have no right to issue proclamations as to what constitutes or does not constitute art fit for Christians to enjoy. I particularly shun any suggestion that the only art glorifying to God is angelically celestial or, in any narrow sense of the word, religious. An orchestral work—*The Seasons* by Vivaldi, Copland's *Appalachian Spring*, or Sibelius' Symphony No. 4 in A minor—can lift the spirit without direct reference to the gospel. Albert Bierstadt's magnificent painting of Mount Rainier can inspire us equally as well as Gerard Manley Hopkins's poem with visions of God's grandeur. There will always be artists whose experience is not necessarily Christian but whose gift, through common grace, enables them to tell as much truth as they know. There are also artists whose vision is distorted, whose purposes may even be debased, whose art is thereby twisted and maimed. Yet from them too, in spite of decadence and corruption, we may obtain momentary vestiges of truth. As Madeleine L'Engle has said, "We can't tell God where he can or can't be seen."

Furthermore, because a knowledge of Jesus Christ includes a recognition of sin, Christians are acutely sensitive to the effects of sin and ought to be able to account for its reality in their art. For a Christian, aesthetics is more than an appreciation of the beautiful; a Christian can also understand why ugliness and anguish must be present in art, as they are present in life. The Christian inhabits the real world—not a world utterly given over to despair, but since the Fall, no longer entirely a garden of earthly delights. Thus, the art a Christian makes and experiences should give both adequate cause and reason for the hope by which his life is steered.

But an awareness of sin's wretchedness presents a problem for the artist, as John Timmerman points out.

> On the one hand we may not neglect the reality of sin and must capture a voice and a vision which will give eloquent testimony to another and higher way. On the other hand we may not become so involved in consideration of sin that we fall subject to it and become spokesmen for it.

This is the special concern of Christians whose vocation requires them to tread that razor's edge between being "in the world" and being "of the world." It is not an easy task, and the person who can fulfill his vocation in the arts without becoming soiled by sin is rare indeed. Only the power of the Holy Spirit can protect; only the forgiveness of Jesus Christ can cleanse.

Why is it necessary to risk contamination in the pollution of popular culture? Because no teacher of literature, for example, can confine his reading to novels by Grace Livingston Hill; no art historian can be content with madonnas and altarpieces; and so on, throughout the arts and sciences. No biologist or medical doctor can afford to ignore the papers documenting research and experimentation in cloning, genetic transfer, abortion, or artificial insemination. He may disapprove of such practices, but he cannot be unfamiliar with them and expect to retain his prophetic witness against them. The same is true for pastors and Sunday school teachers, and especially for parents. We cannot safely guide our congregation, our pupils, or the members of our family if we deliberately choose to remain ignorant of the allurements that would ensnare us all. We must not imitate the three monkeys who, while they speak no evil, also hear and see none either. We must read, listen to, and observe enough of popular culture's entertainment to enjoy what is profitable and warn against what is harmful.

While sampling popular culture, we must avoid becoming trapped ourselves. In St. Paul's startling description of godlessness, at the beginning of his Letter to the Romans, his catalogue of depravity includes not only "those who behave like this," but also those who "applaud such practices" (Romans 1:32). We have long known that sin corrupts without acknowledging any distinction between active and passive participants. This means that what is sinful to *do* is also sinful to enjoy *being done* by somebody else. An exhibitionist needs an audience of voyeurs, and there is no separating the innocent from the guilty. To maintain a proper balance between cultural ignorance and overindulgence calls for spiritual maturity of the highest order. But the gravest danger lurks just at the point when we suppose we have attained that objective. Spiritual maturity is progressive; it leads from step to step, developing as we grow in grace. To be mature means to find room for further growth. As St. Paul said,

> It is not to be thought that I have already achieved all this. I have not yet reached perfection, but I press on, hoping to take hold of that for which Christ once took hold of me (Philippians 3:12).

But if we are ever to make such a discovery—if we are to mature as Christians in our experience with artists and their art—we must begin by leaving behind in the nursery those toys and attitudes of our spiritual infancy. "When I was a child," St. Paul writes, "my speech, my outlook, and my thoughts were all childish. When I grew up, I had finished with childish things" (1 Corinthians 13:11).

The surest way to abandon childishness is to become a *critic*. Unfortunately, common usage of the word narrows our understanding of what it means to be a critic. Negative connotations limit the critic to being someone who delights in pointing out the faults in everyone else's work. Not so. To be a critic means to be capable of discernment—thus the word is used to describe the penetrating keenness of the Word of God in Hebrews 4:12. To be a critic means being skilled to appreciate and evaluate, compare and contrast a work of art and thereby judge its worth. No novice qualifies as a critic. You cannot see your first play or film, or read your first poem, and presume to judge its merits beyond an elementary level of *like* or *dislike*. Criticism develops by weighing this work of art—this opera or painting, this gourmet dish or architect's design—against many similar works, measuring this artist's performance or product against a standard already set by his predecessors and contemporaries. A beginner must reserve judgment until fuller experience with art gives him a basis on which to form his opinion.

A careful shopper acts as a critic, whether looking for the best economy and flavor in a can of coffee, or the best appearance in a dress or suit, or the best buy in a used car. But some of us are wholly ignorant about automobiles; we can do little more than kick the tires and admire the upholstery. So, if we're wise and want to avoid being taken for a sucker, we ask an informed, experienced shopper to go along with us to the used car lot; we want someone who knows cars and whose opinion we respect to serve as a critic of our choices. This critic differs from us in that he knows the right questions to ask, questions that will make an informed decision possible.

Any responsible critic gains his right to make evaluations by asking hard questions of every work claiming a place as art. A critic takes nothing for granted, accepts no opinion at its face value or for its own sake; but a responsible critic also always remembers that his aesthetic judgments—however mature his taste—are no more than personal opinions. *"De gustibus non disputandum est,"* says the philosopher, which being interpreted might say, "My qualified opinions are as good as, but no better than, the next fellow's." The purpose in asking questions is not to assert or prove one's own artistic superiority, but to lead to a decision. By sifting wheat from chaff, by refining gold from dross, the critic is able to decide what is worthy and what is unworthy of his time, energy, emotional attachment, and—in the case of purchase—money.

In discerning the value of a work of art, a critic is asking simultaneously several kinds of questions. Each area of inquiry is a means of reaching out for an understanding of the work as it presents itself to the particular critic's interests. No absolute separation is possible, of course; one cannot hear a piano concerto and listen only for the playing of the black keys. But as a means of discussing the critical process, we may reasonably speak of the critic's search in three areas: He inquires aesthetically, religiously, and as a Christian.

If the critic were examining a machine, his primary interest might well be efficiency; his questions would try to determine how well the machine functions and how little it costs per unit. But in examining a work of art, a critic's first questions will be questions of form, structure, organic independence, integrity, beauty, and style. The critic will be looking at the work *aesthetically*, asking questions such as these:

What holds this work together? What gives it unity, strength, composition?

Does this work give shape or vision to any elements of life otherwise closed off from us?

Does it reveal to us, by representation or by imagination, hidden dimensions of reality?

Is there a freshness to the language, a new rhythm, a new design, a new shape, a new vision? Or has it all been said before, at least as well?

At the same moment the critic is putting these questions forward—and growing directly from his attempt to analyze aesthetically—the critic will also be asking other questions. These probe the level of seriousness which the work represents.

Is it glib and shallow and trivial?

Is it part of a current fad, inconsequential in value?

Or does it participate as a particular realization of a universal truth?

If so, how does this incarnation of cosmic reality affect its viewers or listeners?

When a critic asks these questions, and others related to these concerns, he is looking at a work of art *religiously*. Not in the usual sense of the word, as applied to sect or denomination, creed or cult, but in the sense of commitment to essential principles by which one may order his life. In short, to treat an artist's work religiously means to inquire into his system of values.

A third approach to art takes priority over the other two and goes beyond asking questions of aesthetic worth or religious values. Whenever a Christian confronts works purporting to be art, he addresses ultimate issues of moral and spiritual correspondence. For a work of art must tell us more than questions of aesthetics or seriousness of purpose can answer. A work of art must also account for living realities of loss and gain, despair and hope, guilt and grace. A mature Christian must weigh these factors upon a scale established by Jesus Christ.

In teaching his disciples about the coming of the Holy Spirit, Jesus specified what the work of the Spirit would be: "When he comes, he will confute the world, and show where wrong and right and judgement lie" (John 16:8). Since the Spirit speaks most directly through Christians in whom he dwells, it must be Christians who do this work of the Spirit. It must be Christians who overturn the secular world's accepted standards, pointing out what is both corrupt and sound in our culture, and showing how to judge between the two. Throughout this process of Spirit-led discrimination, Christians must draw all their powers of discernment from the very source of wisdom, the Eternal Logos himself, for Jesus said of the Spirit, "He will glorify me, for everything that he makes known to you he will draw from what is mine" (John 16:14).

The responsibility of every Christian is to be a critic, and the way to look at art—altering slightly Harry Blamires's phrase—is to *look Christianly*. We must try to see as a Christian, hear as a Christian, perceive with all our senses as a Christian; in short, to see as Jesus Christ himself might see. When we look Christianly at art, some of the questions we ask may be these:

> How does the truth about Creation and Incarnation speak through the form and purpose of this work of art?
>
> How does my understanding of the Good News affect the ways in which I respond to this work?
>
> What does this work reveal about the artist's understanding of his vocation?

Theologians and philosophers may ask their questions in slightly different terms. What is the artist's *weltanschauung*, his world-and-life view? What is the platform on which the artist stands to look out and see the world?

This metaphor of vision and stance has been widely popularized without at the same time being well understood. Perhaps an analogy with politics will help. Before a

Presidential election in this country, each political party convenes its delegates to select candidates to present to the electorate. But before these candidates are chosen, a pre-convention session meets at which the leaders of the party draft its principles, its programs to be offered to the voters. This document expresses what the party believes will best suit the common good of the nation. The document is called the party *platform*, and the candidate who runs for election as a representative of the Democratic or Republican party must stand upon that platform—which means he must affirm that he too sees the state of the nation and the solutions to its problems from the vantage of his party's platform. This becomes an articulation of his political view of the world.

So too for the artist, the teacher, the lawyer, physician, or soldier; so for the astronomer or zoologist, for every human being. We choose our place to stand, the vantage point that gives us our view of the world. If that point of view—to illustrate briefly—should overlook the foulest garbage dump, we may well be possessed by a singular vision of the world as trash; if we take our stand upon the parapet of a maximum security penitentiary, we adopt a view of the world as a prison and its inhabitants as inmates; or we may see the world as a cosmic casino in which we are all subject to the vagaries of chance; or we may stand looking through a glass into the dayroom of a mental institution and see the world as an insane asylum; or sit on the rim of a vast stadium and observe the world as a game or race in which we are divided into winners and losers.

But whatever the point of vantage, it must provide us with an unbroken view of the world. St. Paul described as spiritually immature those who are "tossed by the waves and whirled about by every fresh gust of teaching" (Ephesians 4:14). In the apostle's metaphors we see that immaturity is related to instability, the failure to find a firm and fixed place to stand; instead, the immature are subject to every external pressure upon them. It's rather difficult, if not impossible, to see life with any degree of accuracy from the perspective of a drowning man or, as the song says, "Drifting along with the tumbling tumbleweed."

How different is Matthew Arnold's description of the Greek playwright Sophocles, "who saw life steadily, and saw it whole." No wonder his plays have endured for twenty-five centuries! To see life in the wholeness of vision means to see the truth about life. Every artist who hopes to produce work of lasting quality must see to it that his art speaks the truth about human experience—the responsibility of human relationships, the accountability of every human being to the hierarchies of the universe. In order to find this wholeness, this integrity, the artist must first find his place to stand; then he must test his principles to be sure they do indeed provide a view of life that is both responsible and accountable. Anything less results in distorted vision and a fragmented, broken image of human experience.

Nobody understands better than the Marxists the significance of a unified world view, which in their clumsiness they try to impose. In East Germany, for instance, the politburo has been diligent about instructing its citizens in the prescribed view of the German Democratic Republic. Recently, however, the government has become aware that some editors and publishers, not yet members of the Communist Party, may not be adhering closely enough to the single vision of the Party, especially with regard to the novels they publish. The solution? Send these editors and publishers on "educational retreats" so that they can become better equipped to fulfill their responsibilities to the State.

But what awaits these editors and publishers after their indoctrination? What kind of novels will their firms publish? What art is in store for new generations of Germans in their Marxist-socialist paradise? The consequences for art under tyranny, whether political or intellectual, are always the same. Propaganda replaces truth, bias impairs vision, and oppression squelches the imagination. For merely having a point of view from which to see the world is not enough, especially when the point of view adopted constricts into conformity and spiritual enslavement. This is evil at its worst—man's denial of God leading to a usurping of divine prerogatives; declaring himself and his followers omnipotent to determine the nature and quality of human existence as one vast monolith. But such men are blind leading the blind, slaves to their own bondage. Denial of God means that a human being is spiritually crippled—blind, deaf, and dumb—cut off from the source of light and, like the Apocalyptic city of Babylon, doomed to hear no more "the sound of harpers and minstrels, of flute-players and trumpeters" (Revelation 18:22).

What, then, of a Christian world view? The Christian takes his stand, as Jacques Maritain declares, "right at the joining of the arms of the Cross. It is the only place from which one can see well." True freedom belongs to those who see without obstruction. From the vantage of the Cross the Christian holds all of life in clear perspective, sees the whole panorama of God's Creation. A Christian does not stand aloof from the reality he observes; a Christian is not an indifferent commentator at some distant remove from mundane problems afflicting others. A Christian participates in all of life, its suffering and its joy. This integral relationship with what a Christian sees, therefore, is what the artist who is a Christian must portray. For a Christian, art cannot be discrete from the things of the spirit. Its music must reverberate in consonance with the chords of human experience; its language must communicate both the woe and delight of knowing that we are dust made in the image of God.

Near the end of Shakespeare's play *The Merchant of*

Venice, Lorenzo speaks to his bride, Jessica, about the music which surrounds them.

> Here will we sit, and let the sounds of music
> Creep in our ears—soft stillness and the night
> Become the touches of sweet harmony.

He points first at the stars and rhapsodizes on the music of the spheres, unheard by mortals.

> There's not the smallest orb which thou behold'st
> But in his motion like an angel sings,
> Still quiring to the young-eyed cherubims;
> Such harmony is in immortal souls,
> But whilst this muddy vesture of decay
> Doth grossly close it in, we cannot hear it.

Just then, the court musicians begin to play, and Lorenzo gives Jessica one of the clearest definitions of the broken link between art and the things of the spirit.

> The man that hath no music in himself,
> Nor is not moved with concord of sweet sounds,
> Is fit for treasons, stratagems, and spoils,
> The motions of his spirit are dull as night,
> And his affections dark as Erebus.
> Let no such man be trusted. Mark the music.

To look Christianly means to "mark the music." Not to see whether or not the music makes any orthodox statement about theology; not to attempt to define the art as being "Christian" or "non-Christian," *above* or *below* some arbitrary line drawn by our own canons of thinking; none of these. To see Christianly, we need nothing less than the eyes of Christ. But looking through those eyes will not require us to wrest art from its natural state in the world; nor must we try somehow to sanctify art by analysis in biblical or theological terms. Art is its own witness to the fact declared by St. Paul in one of the most liberating texts in Scripture: We worship the God "who endows us richly with all things to enjoy" (1 Timothy 6:17).

At the same time, however, accompanying any such promise of liberty must be a critical awareness of responsibility—the responsibility, for example, to evaluate a work of art in its ethical context, in its historical matrix; to regard it in relation to other contemporary artistic forms; and to do so with the integrity of a qualified observer rather than an anthologizer of other people's criticism. And so, while I cannot support those who claim to be able to distinguish a Christian color or Christian tone or Christian form from its unsanctified counterpart, I do believe that some kinds of art—programmatic art especially—have roots too deep in negative contexts to serve Christ, except as negative examples. I recall with a sense of irony an expensive multi-media presentation at the 1974 Lausanne Congress on World Evangelization, a sound-and-light show opening with the now familiar chords of Richard Strauss's *Also Sprach Zarathustra*—the *2001* music for moviegoers. I wonder what the pagan Friedrich Nietzsche's reaction would be if he knew how far afield his superman thesis had miscarried, by means of the music of the Nazi collaborator Strauss? Surely it had been misappropriated in attempting to underscore a challenge to evangelize the world for Jesus Christ!

Looking Christianly means beaming upon a work of art the spotlight of a critical mind whose judgments are being redeemed by the love of Jesus Christ for a sinful world; whose discernment is being perfected by the grace that makes it possible to say, " 'Christ Jesus came into the world to save sinners,' and among them I stand first" (1 Timothy 1:15). Looking Christianly, therefore, calls forth responses of love, compassion, empathy, and understanding even for artists whose work offends, not to mention those whose attempts at art seem to merit little if any critical comment at all. By looking Christianly, through the lenses of spiritual discernment, we can learn to appreciate a composition in stone, a blend of colors or ingredients, a harmony of flowers, a poem in gymnastics, or a ballet of courtesy in our own homes. For whenever a Christian looks closely enough at art, he can hardly fail to find—as the Bauhaus architect Mies van der Rohe has said—proof that "God is in the details."

Wrestling with the Word

Sitting daily at this desk and typewriter—surrounded by scattered papers overflowing onto the floor at my feet, threatened by piles of books about to topple—I sometimes ask myself what I am doing or trying to do. Moments of healthy introspection, as well as other moments of self-doubt and discouragement, have taught me the value of the single answer that throbs in my brain: "I'm writing because my life depends upon it!" You see, I am coming to know this about myself: I write for the same reason I breathe—not because I choose to, but because I'm compelled to write in order to *be*. I breathe in, I breathe out; the experience of life is my inspiration, writing about it my expiration.

I write because, as the poet says, "It is in me and will out!" I have no other choice. I am a writer for the same reason that other men and women are florists or acrobats or slalom racers or truck drivers—because nothing else brings me the same kind of joy as knowing that I am fulfilling my vocation, the personal calling I have received from God to serve him.

To some observers, the vocation of writing appears to be little more than what Goethe called "busy idleness"—a description I reject as pure rot. Yet I can understand how it might be possible to misconstrue a writer's labor as frivolous self-indulgence. He sits at a desk facing a blank sheet of paper and making irregular jottings or typing forays upon the page. But the writer gives little or no evidence of *working* in the same sense that a sculptor works or a chef works or a motion picture director works. Each of them appears to deal with materials and objects commanding public attention and recognition as works of art—a block of stone or a piece of steel becoming a statue, an array of fresh vegetables becoming a salad, a contingent of actors and technicians putting together a film. In such company, the writer is at a public disadvantage, for the medium with which the writer works is impalpable. It is language, whose roots are in the soul, not in the dictionary—language which must be mined, its ore extracted, its gold refined, its dross discarded. Often a writer's only tangible proof that he has been at work will be the crumpled pages filling his wastebasket.

And so, to compensate, sometimes the writer adopts a self-deprecating attitude. For a number of years, before I knew and dared to declare my vocation, my summers between school terms were spent as a closet writer. Friends and colleagues were all active and productive in the usual summer employment of teachers—as camp supervisors or tutors. When neighbors would inquire of me, "What are you doing this summer?" I would whine in reply, "Oh, I'm just writing." Then I would slink away, hating myself for so despising my work that others could only despise it also. Over the years, my wife and children have given me immeasurable support; but there was a time at the beginning when I am sure my wife wondered how the next trip to the supermarket would be paid and why I didn't get a job like other teachers in summer. To this day, certain of my acquaintances have no understanding of the fact that the sound of my typewriter in action means that I am at work and not available for light conversation.

It's not unusual, therefore, to find a writer withdrawn from society, introverted at public gatherings, ill at ease except when engrossed in his work. Some of the most disabled public speakers we may ever hear are writers out of their proper element. The writer knows that he is a solitary creature; his art demands what Wordsworth called "the bliss of solitude." He is a writer, not a member of a committee. His mission is to *write*, not to produce an abomination of group-think or any other collectivized propaganda. To perform his task well, the writer must work alone. He must accustom himself to his own companionship, to the inevitable loneliness of his vocation. He has no other choice because in order to write what is within him—and what else is there to write?—the writer must plunge down the narrow shaft of his personality. There he may find profundities of thought from which to draw, but he can only reach those wide caverns by inching through the passages of his soul; and this must be done alone and as regularly as breathing.

But there is never anything easy about art, least of all the art of writing, which T. S. Eliot calls "the intolerable wrestle/ With words and meanings." The poet's metaphor of physical exertion and struggle brings to mind the patriarch Jacob, who would not let go of God until he had received the promise of blessing. A Christian who writes or paints or sings—whatever his art—must be prepared to do no less than Jacob. The artist cannot afford to believe any of those stories about somebody else who just sat down and spun out a tapestry without even breaking into a sweat. It simply does not happen that way. The making of art is hard work.

No one has yet devised a way whereby art can ignite like flames from spontaneous combustion. To be an artist requires discipline, a nasty word in this age of easy-does-it. But let the word go forth: Easy-does-it-not! Like life itself, there can be no true art that is not born in pain and labor. Anything else is ersatz, phony, less than the genuine article. To be an artist requires commitment to agonizing hours of physical energy and willingness to endure both the body's aches and the mind's weariness. To become an artist, one must know his vocation and practice it—not occasionally or as the itch demands or when convenient or when the mood takes or when everything else is tranquil and the time is right. The violinist Mischa Elman knew the necessity of consistent, daily discipline in his art. He said, "If I miss one day of practice, I know; if I miss two days, my wife knows; but if I miss three days, the world knows."

There's no getting around the fact that any aspiring artist must be prepared to wrestle with the medium he hopes to fashion into a work of art. A painter must wrestle with the mix of colors and varieties of brush strokes; a composer of music wrestles with tone quality, meter, dynamics, and other elements of sound; a writer, as Eliot says, wrestles "with words and meanings." As long ago as the beginning of the second century A.D., the Roman philosopher Epictetus said, "If you wish to be a writer, write." That summons is to the daily grind, a schedule that calls just as surely as any other vocation makes its demands.

I believe that it was Jacques Barzun who said, "Most young men have no desire to *write*; they prefer to *have written*." He is referring to the pleasure one feels at seeing one's own name in a byline or on a dust jacket. It *is* a good feeling, but how did that name get there? By analogy, it is the same way in which a champion athlete finds his or her name in the record books—by dint of labor, self-denial, dull but necessary repetition of skills, the kind of plodding drudgery that forms a foundation upon which to build. As a writer, I can testify to days, weeks, even months of toil the like of which no ditch-digger can equal. "Composition," said Samuel Johnson, "is, for the most part, an effort of slow diligence and steady perseverance, to which the mind is dragged by necessity or resolution." To which Jonathan Swift adds this practical advice:

Blot out, correct, insert, refine,
Enlarge, diminish, interline;
Be mindful, when invention fails,
To scratch your head, and bite your nails.

When the writing is actually completed and the writer's energies are fully spent, he may feel almost as breathless as a marathon runner at the finish of his ordeal.

But before I offend too many behavioral psychologists with my metaphor of breath and spirit, let me add that, however arduous, the act of writing is also an attempt to bring order out of the chaos of my life. Like everyone else, I am a prisoner in time and space, shackled to a schedule of conflicting demands, forced to submit to laws of gravity and entropy. Whirling about me are persons and events in apparent randomness. "While I talk," said William James, "and the flies buzz, a sea gull catches a fish at the mouth of the Amazon, a tree falls in the Adirondack wilderness, a man sneezes in Germany, a horse dies in Tartary, and twins are born in France." Then James went on to ask, "What does that mean? Does the contemporaneity of these events with one another, and with a million others as disjointed, form a rational bond between them, and unite them into anything that means for us a world?" Disorder and accident, circumstance and coincidence seem to be the program for modern living—a fact so disturbing to some people, they take refuge in political or psychological management of human beings, hoping thereby to curb the unpredictable element and root out the mystery of human nature.

Art in general, the art of writing in particular, provides a better way of bringing order to existence than either political or psychological control. Manufacturers of patent medicines offer panaceas like Compoz. Art offers *composition*—the orderly arrangement of shrubs, oils, notes, words, or atoms to form some shape. The tangle of growth and undergrowth becomes a landscaped garden; the cacophony of sound becomes music; a crazy quilt of ideas, half-formed and inarticulate, becomes a poem or a manual on the repair of washing machines. Although the slang cliche of the *Hair* generation has long since dissipated itself, its truth remains: Composition means "getting your head together."

Of course, I have been assuming a definition of art and composition whose purpose *is* to bring order out of chaos. But I also recognize that much of the alleged art of our time seems anything but orderly. The music Pierre Boulez intends to make in the future, he claims, cannot even be written down. But no matter how aleatory such music may appear, the fact is that it does not go on in a vacuum forever; a certain slice of time, a specific place, and a determinable number of performers and listeners are involved. These factors frame the experience and impose upon it an order called selectivity. It is not the whole of acoustical science; it is a fragment fixed in time and space. So too with the so-called paintings of the most bizarre conceptualists. Rudolph Schwarzkogler's castration and Chris Burden's crucifixion to the rooftop of a Volkswagen minibus are selected instances of suicidal mania, frozen in time and space. Whether ironically or not, however, they constitute a degree of order in an otherwise antinomian and nihilistic environment; for they bring to artist and audience alike selected instances of human derangement. With no pun intended, such art is composition in the midst of decomposition, affirmation growing out of negation, the paradox of belief in the face of disbelief. For it is assertive of at least one sure reality, the fact of death, and the human struggle to overcome the Last Enemy by one means or another.

In somewhat less dramatic terms, I suppose, my daily act of writing is like the man in Stephen Crane's poem, addressing the universe with the fact of individual existence.

> A man said to the universe,
> "Sir, I exist."

The writer is not in the least disturbed when the universe replies,

> "However, . . .
> The fact has not created in me
> A sense of obligation."

Such indifference may be the very challenge the writer has been waiting for! The poem—this act of recording a universal affront to human dignity and worth—this very piece of writing—is its own testament to human consciousness, even in the face of such apparent cosmic disdain.

So, writing is an affirmation of personal identity; but it is also a means of ordering one's own universe. As William Faulkner put it in his Nobel Prize speech:

> The poet's voice need not merely be the record of man, it can be one of the props, the pillars to help him endure and prevail.

The written word supports our society in much the same manner that the retelling of tribal myth around the village fire upholds an aboriginal culture. But for writing to succeed as a prop or pillar, it must possess the dignity of its art; it cannot be reduced to the level of a technical skill—like the classes in "Business English" taught in adult education programs. If writing is an attribute of my humanness, it ought to be elevated to its proper place as both a discipline of human rationality and a celebration of human spirituality. To be able to write is a token of my uniqueness among the creatures of the universe. As a teacher, I must never abuse this gift by compelling others to write as punishment; rather, I must show my students that writing, like the taking of home movies, is a way of fixing a lasting impression of life's experiences. Writing today provides a record for tomorrow—a verbal cross-section of my thought preserved out of the concatenation of life's events.

I write because I must; I write because I find order to my life through expression and communication. But buried in that last remark is a key word: the verb *find*. I *find* order. It does not come laid out for me like a Simplicity dress pattern or a set of blueprints. Finding order through writing is an adventure in discovery.

Any genuine artist is on a journey from Here to Somewhere. He is possessed by a continually surging discontent with his present situation. "What's my favorite song?" replied the late Duke Ellington to an interviewer. "The next one, the one I haven't written yet." The artist who takes his work seriously never resorts to formula solutions to problems arising in his art. He is never satisfied to repeat what worked the last time. Instead, he is perpetually in quest of those mercies of God, granted through common grace, that are new every morning—a new song, a new sight, a new taste, a new texture, a new perception of reality, a new respect for the natural order, a new joy in the fullness of life.

One of the most serious hindrances to the effective teaching of writing in our schools—perhaps in our colleges and universities as well—is the typical teacher's contempt for the mystery of discovery. How often was I told in writing courses that my outline would be due on such a day and my essay, due sometime later, would be checked against my outline. What madness! It makes as much sense as requiring Ferdinand Magellan to present a ship's log before his voyage. Most of the joy of sightseeing in a great museum can be spoiled by a too-fixed attention to the guidebook instead of allowing one's feet to wander where the eye leads.

The writer, like those explorers whose names we celebrate, sets out on a journey with only the vaguest sense of where it may lead. Of course, the writer is accompanied on his journey by the spirits of those who have preceded him, for no artist is free from influences upon him. Yet the writer hopes to chart a new course, showing some facet of nature or of human nature previously undisclosed to us. The light of his art, he hopes, will illumine darkened corners of our experience. Not novelty, for novelty serves no purpose in art; it is sheer exhibitionism, the product of "hype" and sensation. To be a writer means to explore those undiscovered territories of the spirit.

Every writer needs a compass to determine direction; every writer also needs the humility to backtrack when intuition and good sense—not to mention a knowledge of rhetoric, logic, semantics—dictate the wisdom of returning to the road not taken. George Booth, the *New Yorker* cartoonist, readily admits that when drawing a five-panel strip, he rarely knows what his people and animals will be saying or doing by the end of the cartoon. He finds out as he draws them. Humphrey Carpenter, Tolkien's biographer, writes that when Tolkien was asked what his poems meant, he replied, "I don't know. I'll try to find out." Carpenter says that Tolkien "did not see himself as an inventor of story, but as a discoverer of legend." Joan Didion tells an interviewer, "Writing a novel is like telling myself a story. The story makes itself up as it goes along. . . . You never really know where it's going until you're in the last part." Arthur Miller says, "If I know the end of a story, I can't write it because there's nothing to discover." To which E. M. Forster would add, "How can I tell what I think till I see what I say?"

Yet the writer also knows by experience a profound mystery. He knows that the farther he pursues the hint of a new theme, the more probable it is that he will find himself having come round full circle to the base from which he started. "The end is where we start from," wrote T. S. Eliot in the final of his *Four Quartets;* then he went on to say,

> We shall not cease from exploration
> And the end of all our exploring
> Will be to arrive where we started
> And know the place for the first time.

Every real writer knows this to be true, although in the heat of his lonely struggle, the writer may also see himself engaged in bailing a sinking boat, in backing-and-filling against floods of indifference to language and literature. Beyond the sham of our society's sophisticated loquacity lie chasms of cultural void. No one who cares about traditions of civilized discourse could dispute the fact that we are becoming a continent of deliberate fools, benighted and loving it, cynical, illiterate, anti-intellectual philistines of such gigantic ignorance that we could only be sons of Goliath.

We have become a nation deafened by pandemonium, hoarse from the sound of our own shouting. Our tongues waggle ceaselessly, but say almost nothing. On television talk shows, the level of language frequently resembles an exchange between inmates of Bedlam. Even worse are the telephone dialogues on radio, with their banality, their ill-considered opinions, their unremitting flow of clichés, their mindless repetition of received wisdom. Listening, one could almost wish for a nationwide plague of dumbness to strike us all. T. S. Eliot's common man Sweeney speaks for many when he tells his girl friend Doris,

I gotta use words when I talk to you
But if you understand or if you dont
That's nothing to me and nothing to you
We all gotta do what we gotta do.

But while some critics of language use in America are in despair over our present conditions, students of animal behavior are ecstatic over new triumphs. At the Yerkes Institute in Atlanta, Georgia, they have a most remarkable primate, a chimpanzee named Lana. According to *The New York Times*, Lana has learned to speak: that is, she has learned to arrange the words and phrases in her programmed vocabulary into elementary sentences punched out on her computerized typewriter.

Behavioral scientists are already hailing Lana's feat as a major victory over the reactionary forces of humanism and supernatural theism. "See," they chortle, "man isn't so special after all. He's merely *homo sapiens*, the human animal, a biped without feathers. He's really no different from other animals."

Of course, I'm not surprised by this news from Atlanta. Lana's not the first female whose use of language has made monkeys out of men! But I am afraid I must demur from applauding the chimp's accomplishments, however amazing they may seem. I once saw a dog that would bow its head and fold its forepaws whenever its master said, "Our Father . . . ," but I never considered that to be prayer. One of the basic misconceptions about language is that its primary function is *communication*. But *communication* as such is a sterile, innocuous word, a word without sufficient shape to give it character. Yes, both the chimp and the fox terrier may be communicating in response to other communicators; but what both animals lack—and what no human being can avoid—is the moral dimension in language.

The way we view language depends wholly on the

way we view the human race. The metaphor of a world-and-life view again serves to describe the vantage point from which we stand to look out and see the world. Some people see the human race as an accident, random and uncaused, a biochemical freak that somehow developed, no one knows how. For these observers, the utterances made by the human specimen are as meaningless as the question *Why?* Others see man as the product of a vast universal assembly line, a wondrously intricate machine. To them, his squeaks and coughs, his cries and whispers are merely what the scientific reductionist calls them—programmed responses of the human mechanism intelligible to certain other human machines. Or perhaps humankind may be considered as a higher grade of natural being, evolved after long passage through the slime and sloughing off, until at last, by a monumental exertion of will, he arrives at the highest point so far on the ascending scale, possessing—though from what source no one can say—both a mind and the capacity for speech. If one accepts any of these naturalistic explanations, then one must also concede that a million monkeys on a million typewriters might very well—in a million years—turn out *Walden Two*, if not Thoreau's original.

There are, of course, other platforms from which to stand and see the world, other criteria by which to judge the uniqueness of man. But whatever its source, accompanying the phenomenon of language goes a complementary obligation imposed only upon human beings. Dogs may bark, lions roar, and chimpanzees perform their cybernetic circus acts. But only the human being is responsible for what he says. Man alone holds other men accountable for pledges, promises, vows, oaths, and even for slips of the tongue. In fact, we well judge the moral character of a person simply by the response to this question: "Is she—is he—as good as his word?"

The moral dimension of language will always serve to

measure a society's moral condition. In our society, the moral condition may best be observed in the manipulation of language by ad men for J. Walter Thompson or BBD & O. Our most influential *communicators*—to use their favorite self-description—are copywriters shaped by human engineers into experts in equivocation. With increasing frequency, their skills of obfuscation and doubletalk equip them to be retooled for government positions of power; thereafter, the bureaucratic casuistry they practice compels them to tell the people only what they want us to hear. In doing so, these advocates of George Orwell's "newspeak" customarily change the primary meanings of words, rendering them inoperative at any convenience. Surely Shakespeare knew the tricks of Madison Avenue and of Washington, D. C., when he gave Banquo these words of warning for Macbeth:

> . . . oftentimes to win us to our harm
> The instruments of darkness tell us truths,
> Win us with honest trifles, to betray us
> In deepest consequence.

Ralph Waldo Emerson wrote, "Use what language you will, you can never say anything but what you are." What we are, our use of language betrays, as Simon Peter learned to his sorrow. Jesus had already taught that "the words that the mouth utters come from the overflowing of the heart" (Matthew 12:34). Language is character, which is a far deeper truth than the rhetorical adage that says, "The style is the man." No matter how earnestly we strive to cover up, the conscience-driven Claudius, king of Denmark, speaks for us all in a brief soliloquy:

> The harlot's cheek, beautied with plastering art,
> Is not more ugly to the thing that helps it
> Than is my deed to my most painted word.

Shakespeare's metaphor is striking. The consequences of her harlotry break out upon the prostitute's face in syphilitic sores. To cover her ugliness and keep herself in business, she reaches for her Revlon or Max Factor make-up kit; she smears her face and returns to her trade. In a moment of rare, honest self-examination, Hamlet's uncle sees himself for the hypocrite he is—a foul betrayer and murderer whose awful deed remains despite the layers of cosmetic language he piously intones. His own words condemn him for his sin.

The writer holds a paradoxical position in modern life. For the greater part of his days, he is subjected to a blind uncaringness of the masses, whose use of language reflects the disdain for verbal precision they have learned from advertising. The public's apparent predilection for clichés and jargon eliminates any possibilities of style and meaning from intruding upon the manipulation and abuse of words. But every so often, the writer is confronted by a challenge from society to say exactly what he means, to talk in plain English. Then comes his greater despair, for he can almost never hope to describe to the careless mob the limits of language—that vast disparity between emotion and expression, the difference between his interior vision of truth and its external representation. To the philistine who knows no such dilemma—who prides himself on always saying exactly what's on his mind!—the writer appears a fool, a hypersensitive aesthete, a dandy no better than J. Alfred Prufrock, whose lament brings scorn rather than sympathy when he cries, "It is impossible to say just what I mean!"

In this loneliness the writer experiences another frustration, an almost daily realization that the language he labored so hard to master yesterday has slipped out of his grasp today; or the phrases that seemed so appropriate then are now outdated. Eliot also knew this quandary:

> Trying to learn to use words, and every attempt
> Is a wholly new start, and a different kind of failure

Because one has only learnt to get the better of words
For the thing one no longer has to say, or the way in which
One is no longer disposed to say it. And so each venture
Is a new beginning, a raid on the inarticulate
With shabby equipment always deteriorating
In the general mass of imprecision of feeling,
Undisciplined squads of emotion.

This is when the writer knows that he is at war not only against forces of illiteracy and verbal oppression, but also at war against discouragement and a loss of faith in his vocation.

Sometimes the sternest opposition to a writer comes from those who might have been expected to give their support—fellow-Christians who have not yet developed a spiritual understanding of language or art. They are still under the influence of secularism and popular culture, in which language is bandied about for materialistic purposes. Immature Christians, as well as disbelievers, have not yet understood the sublime nature of language, its dynamism, its organic reality; they do not comprehend the relationship between language and life or recognize the moral dimension of language. Why? Because they do not recognize its source in the Eternal Word.

For centuries, rhetoricians and orators, playwrights and poets have searched for some correlation between language and life. In this era of relativism, in this maelstrom of valuelessness, a secular lie prevails, that words are only signs to be pointed in any direction we choose. Like Humpty-Dumpty, many contemporary speakers and writers would claim, "When I use a word, it means just what I choose it to mean—neither more nor less." When such folly rules, confusion cannot be far behind; and with confusion, anarchy. How remarkable, therefore, that when Christians come to know their Creator in a personal relationship, the One who redeems human experience from its meaninglessness is not the Fastest Gun in the West, not the Man of Steel, but the Word-Made-Flesh!

To any writer the preeminence of language must be assumed. For any writer who aspires to be an artist, nothing can be more significant than this statement: "In the beginning was the Word." But for the writer who is also a Christian, who has identified Jesus of Nazareth as "the Christ, the Son of the living God," the corollary is also significant: he knows personally the Word who became flesh. The Incarnation heralds the coming of Good News brought by God's Messenger—the divine Logos, the Liberating Word! The Christian who has been called to be a writer has been granted the high vocation of speaking the word about the Word himself! As part of his calling, the writer who is a Christian has been commissioned to imitate the Creator and Redeemer in calling order out of chaos, in giving form to the formless and meaning to the meaningless. Because of the mystery of the Incarnation, by which the Word became flesh and dwelt among us, the writer has available to him the whole range of human experience expressible in language. He may choose to tell his story directly, in which case he risks appearing didactic and sermonic. If he is more subtle, he will employ some means of indirection—allegory, parable, irony, or paradox, which G. K. Chesterton defined as "truth standing on its head to get attention."

Because the medium of his art is language, a Christian called to be a writer values words as sacraments of the Living Word. Thus, the struggle for excellence is far more than a desire to find the *mot juste* for its own sake. It is, rather, a spiritual desire to reach upward toward the highest standard of expression in word and act. No inscription of any kind—no note or memo or letter—is trivial because every piece of writing, to a Christian, must be another instance of the writer's wrestling with God until light dawns with his blessing.

The Cost of Being a Writer

Most readers are fascinated by a writer and the supposed glamour that surrounds him. they hear about a million-dollar contract issued to Norman Mailer; they read of Truman Capote's power to make or break the mighty with a word; they see the romantic figure of a writer circulating among the beautiful people at a favorite spa; or they recall those careless expatriates lounging in Gertrude Stein's salon. It all seems so grand, so extraordinarily free. "I'd give anything to be a writer," says someone. If that someone is you, then I should talk frankly with you, not about advances and royalties, not about extravagant lunches and publishers' parties, not about the thrill of seeing your name in print, not about the glamour; instead, let's talk about the cost of being a writer.

One of my former teachers, Walker Gibson, has written a poem about the cost of being a writer, called "Epistle to the Reader."

If only I'd quit fooling round with rhyme,
Get down to work for Hollywood, or *Time*
And follow some respectable career,
I could be making forty grand a year
(Or thereabouts), and from some leather chair

Surrounded by a desk an acre square,
While secretaries flounced among their files
Exchanging with their bosses sexy smiles,
I could be buzzing buzzers gainfully,
My finger on the pulse of industry.
Reader: you may think this sounds optimistic.
Still, let's suppose you grant me my statistic.
Then I know what it costs to write this verse—
It costs me twenty bucks an hour, or worse.
(How many people spend that kind of dough
On things like poetry, I'd like to know.)
It's money talks, they say, but I talk too;
I'm paying through the nose to talk to you;
And as for you, it's only fair to mention
You're paying through the nose to pay attention.
We're wild and reckless spenders, you and I;
Relationships like yours and mine come high—
Just call us millionaires! I say it's funny
That life is dearest when it costs us money.

We live in a materialistic age; it's only reasonable, therefore, that we should consider the cost that first comes to mind. Careful, scrupulous writing, like any other art, consumes energy and time; and, as the poet Gibson points out, time is money. Most of us feel that we have to get on with the business of making a living; consequently, in most cases, the art of writing is reduced to a hobby, an avocation; reduced so as not to interfere with our materialistic priorities. In making that decision, we choose the course of least resistance, and the frustration we live with derives from that choice. For art is never satisfied to be an avocation, a resort for dabblers or a refuge for the timid.

And what, then, of the cost? It's perfectly evident that few of us can do two things at once. You can't write while working full-time in a shoe factory, as Tom Wingfield in *The Glass Menagerie* knows. The time comes when the aspiring writer must make a decision between security and his passion, between compromise and the fulfillment of his vocation. When he reaches that point of no return, he must decide either to "lay it on the line," as Hemingway said, or to settle for the realization that he will never be anything more than a frustrated artist.

Happily, there are exceptions to every rule. It is possible for some persons of rare and diversified gifts to practice two vocations at once. The poets Eliot, Wallace Stevens, and William Carlos Williams come to mind. One of New York City's eminent attorneys is the novelist Louis Auchincloss; another novelist, D. Keith Mano, oversees the family cement business, and Madeleine L'Engle is a librarian. We scarcely need to call attention to the friends at Oxford who managed so successfully to combine their various careers as university don, barrister, or publisher with the writing of fiction, poetry, and drama. But as I say, these are exceptions whose prodigious energy and imagination appear to have left them with sufficient resources to accomplish both their art and their other professions in one lifetime. Few of us can hope to emulate them.

But if the writer decides to pay the price, to sacrifice security for the sake of his art, he will find riches no certified public accountant can tabulate. He will find that the adage, "Time is money," works both ways. For if it is true that time spent in writing is time lost for earning wages, then it is also true that time spent in writing is time redeemed from its wastedness in mere wage-earning. Kindly allow me to speak from personal experience for a moment.

Several years ago, after many years of frustration as a sometime-writer—"I'll do it sometime"—I decided that *this* was the time. Since 1958, when I announced to my wife that my summer job had evaporated and that I intended to write rather than look for other employment, I had been a summer writer. With the publication of a few articles resulting from those summer indulgences, I'd begun attempting to fit a pattern of writing into my schedule as a teacher of English, school choir director, track coach, and all the other manifold responsibilities of a boarding school faculty member. Somehow my work got done, and the articles increased; then a book or two—textbooks at first—developed out of my teaching experience. But these were not satisfying enough, and there was too little time. A major decision had to be made.

In God's providence, he gave me a headmaster who possesses a spiritual gift and a useful art called administration—the gift and art of being able to organize and utilize other members of the Body of Christ in an efficient and productive way. I made known my conviction that I could not continue to be a teacher-who-writes; I must become a writer-who-teaches; I must be faithful to the insistent call to exercise my gift. In faith, I was asking for a part-time position at a commensurate salary in exchange for the time to write. My request was granted. The details of my arrangement with The Stony Brook School aren't important, except to point out that, released from regular teaching responsibilities, I found it possible to break the logjam and commit myself to a daily regimen of writing. From time to time this schedule has been altered somewhat, as the needs of my school call for my service; but I am no longer frustrated by wondering what might have happened *if only* I had attempted to become a writer. Nor do I look back with regret or ahead with anxiety, for I have found, with Eliot, that "right action is freedom/ From past and future also." The stewardship of my time today is what matters.

But simply having made a vocational choice to be a writer does not diminish the cost. Writing devours both energy and time, often at inconvenient hours. The strain of writing extends beyond all constitutional limits of "cruel and unusual punishments." It sentences the writer to yield all his available time to the project at hand; it robs him of leisure and vacation, no matter how exotic, for he is never free from thinking, "Wait till I get back home and write about this!" His compulsion to write renders him—in the eyes of his family, at least—into the caricature of a graphomaniac, a person obsessed by a single purpose in living: to write!

A writer knows the impossibility of shutting down the engines, turning off the power, and utterly relaxing. Like Thoreau, whether literally or figuratively, he too keeps a pencil under the pillow so that when he cannot sleep, he writes in the dark. My wife has grown accustomed to my slipping out of bed at crazy times of the night to stave off further sleeplessness caused by an incessant idea that must be put down on paper. To comfort her, I have suggested that she pretend to be Abigail, whose husband, the poet-king, apparently got some of his best lines in the same after-hours manner. For he tells us, in Psalm 16:7, "I will bless the Lord who has given me counsel: in the night-time wisdom comes to me in my inward parts."

But perhaps you are saying, "Why all this special pleading about the price a writer pays? Look at Harold Robbins and Irwin Shaw—they make millions! Look at . . ."—and the list of writers who have struck it rich continues. Even in the special category of so-called "Christian books," there is another whole roster of writers who have been able to praise the Lord all the way to the bank. What does their financial success say about the cost of being a writer?

I speak as one who is thoroughly familiar with the business of writing *worst-sellers*. But before you accuse me of sour grapes, let me say that even my limited experience confirms what I have heard best-selling writers say: The greatest calamity that can befall any artist is the kind of success that cripples his art. He is a writer, he has labored long and lovingly over his art; if he is successful and makes a lot of money and attends a lot of parties and acquires an abundance of luxuries, these can divert him from his art. When the time comes to write another novel or play, the process will not be any different, despite all his wealth and fame, from what it was the first time. Like climbing a mountain, writing is the art of putting one word after another until the goal is reached. Nothing interferes with writing like success, and to be a writer one must be willing to recognize that acclaim is always a snare; popularity is a price too high to pay.

To be a writer costs emotionally as well as materially. Every writer knows the anguish of rejection. If the truth were told, nobody really loves a writer—not if he tells the truth—because we are all afraid that the truth the writer tells will somehow expose some weakness in us. And so, we find it comforting to speak disparagingly about the writer. (When addressing a college audience, I sometimes add, "If you don't believe me, try this experiment: The next time you talk to your girlfriend's parents, especially her father, tell him that you have decided to abandon your career in medicine or engineering to become a poet. Or tell your boyfriend's mother that you expect her son to provide you with a housemaid because you intend to be busy writing plays. Your prospective in-laws' reaction will astonish you!")

Nobody, including his biographers, can really know what events in his life Robert Frost may have been referring to in his poem, "The Road Not Taken." But it is entirely possible that he was speaking about his vocational decision, to give up teaching and farming and devote himself to becoming a poet. The final stanza of that poem is wistful as he says,

> I shall be telling this with a sigh
> Somewhere ages and ages hence;
> Two roads diverged in a wood, and I—

I took the one less traveled by,
And that has made all the difference.

And that has made all the difference—between one road and another, between one course of life and its "less traveled" alternative; the difference between the easy and popular routine of going about the daily round of affairs and the difficult labor of composing poetry; in short, the difference between being a respectable citizen and being a mere poet.

But wasn't Robert Frost our unofficial poet laureate, the favorite of President Kennedy? Didn't he read a poem at the Inaugural Ceremonies? Yes, indeed, and it is wonderful that it happened at all, considering the usual public posture toward poets in America. But read carefully the story of Frost's early career and his rejection as a poet. He retreated to England and published his first books of verse there because in this country he could find no publisher and, he thought, his being a poet would not be such an embarrassment to his family if he were to practice his art overseas.

Quite apart from social rejection is the stigma accompanying the work of the writer whose message is unpopular, whose vocation is a scandal to the complacent public. Such a writer in America was Herman Melville, who persevered in his art, even at the cost of favor. In a moving letter to his friend Nathaniel Hawthorne, Melville wrote,

> Dollars damn me; and the malicious Devil is forever grinning in upon me, holding the door ajar. . . . What I feel most moved to write, that is banned,—it will not pay. Yet, altogether, write the *other* way I cannot.

Melville was referring to the struggle going on within him in that tempestuous summer of 1851, a struggle to break away from what had been for him a successful but dissatisfying form of writing. He had begun with a romanticized travelogue *Typee* and its sequel *Omoo;* then to shipboard adventures, *Redburn* and *White-Jacket*, very popular at the time. He had made one attempt to break away from adventure stories in the metaphysical allegory *Mardi*; it was a disastrous failure. Now Melville faced the problem in writing his current novel: Would he revert to the mere telling of a whopping good tale, a whale of a story? Or would he allow himself to write what he felt most moved to write? You know the decision he made. *Moby-Dick* stands as the greatest imaginative work produced by an American. It is our *Odyssey*, our *Divine Comedy*, our *Paradise Lost*.

What makes *Moby-Dick* a worthy contender among the world's great classics is not only its titanic characters, not its rhetorical symphony, for these are but the means to an author's end. *Moby-Dick* stands with the epics of literature because it dares unflinchingly to tell the truth. Melville knew the risk he was chancing. He had written to Hawthorne,

> . . . Truth is the silliest thing under the sun. Try to get a living by the Truth—and go to the Soup Societies. Heavens! Let any clergyman try to preach the Truth from its very stronghold, the pulpit, and they would ride him out of his church on his own pulpit bannister. . . . Why so? Truth is ridiculous to men.

No wonder, then, that when it was published, *Moby-Dick* was a rejected book, as were all of Melville's subsequent books. When he died forty years later, in 1891, his books were out-of-print; he was virtually a forgotten man. In a trunk lay hidden a manuscript of a story he had despaired of publishing, the beautiful and luminous story of Billy Budd, a narrative of law and grace. W. H. Auden characterizes the aged Melville in his poem:

> . . . he cried in exultation and surrender
> "The Godhead is broken like bread. We are the pieces."
> And sat down at his desk and wrote a story.

But in order to find the inner spiritual calm from which a story like *Billy Budd* might spring, Herman Melville first had to accept the cost of being an honest writer, willing to sacrifice fame and possible fortune for the integrity of writing what he felt "most moved to write."

Yet from that faithfulness to his vocation, Melville was able to draw this consolation, shared with Hawthorne in a typically whimsical mood:

> If ever, my dear Hawthorne, in the eternal times that are to come, you and I shall sit down in Paradise, in some little shady corner by ourselves; and if we shall by any means be able to smuggle a basket of champagne there (I won't believe in a Temperance Heaven), and if we shall then cross our celestial legs in the celestial grass that is forever tropical, and strike our glasses and our heads together, till both musically ring in concert,—then, O my dear fellow-mortal, how shall we pleasantly discourse of all the things manifold which now so distress us,—when all the earth shall be but a reminiscence, yea, its final dissolution in antiquity. Then shall songs be composed as when wars are over; humorous, comic songs,—"Oh, when I lived in that queer little hole called the world," or "Oh, when I toiled and sweated below," or "Oh, when I knocked and was knocked in the fight"—yes, let us look forward to such things. Let us swear that, though now we sweat, yet it is because of the dry heat which is indispensable to the nourishment of the vine which is to bear the grapes that are to give us the champagne hereafter.

Integrity is always worth whatever it may cost, and Herman Melville has his enduring reward.

In our own time, we have been strengthened by the example of a writer willing to pay the full cost of his artistic and moral integrity. I speak, of course, of Aleksandr Solzhenitsyn. In the winter of 1974, he was facing imminent execution; three hours later, he landed in West Germany, an exile stripped of his citizenship in the Soviet Union. What drove Soviet hoodlums to their frenzied, clumsy harassment of a mere scribbler? The whole remarkable story is too complex for telling here, but we do well to recall the irony of Solzhenitsyn's rise and fall as a writer in his own government's good graces. In 1962, *One Day in the Life of Ivan Denisovich* coincided with Nikita Khrushchev's de-Stalinization campaign; thus the short novel was permitted to be published because its spare, laconic portrayal of a prison camp's brutalities and commonplace barbarities provided Chairman Khrushchev with a credible witness against the greatest mass murderer in history.

No doubt the Soviet authorities mistook Solzhenitsyn for an opportunist, a writer who would quickly catch on to the fact that one writes what is convenient for the State to publish. In this they were disappointed, for Solzhenitsyn persisted in writing and smuggling out of Russia the most inconvenient descriptions of ongoing repression and petty bureaucratic suffocation of human rights. Worse, these incendiary works were also being circulated in manuscript form by a dissident underground which would not yield to stifling political pressures.

Following *One Day in the Life* . . . came *The First Circle* and *Cancer Ward*. In spite of Solzhenitsyn's impassioned appeals to the Congress of Soviet Writers, his books were suppressed in his own country. By 1970, when the Swedish Academy awarded him the Nobel Prize in Literature, it was apparent that if he left Russia to accept the prize in Stockholm, he would be denied re-entry. Rather than turn his back on his own nation and people, Solzhenitsyn accepted the honor, but declined to receive the prize itself until a more appropriate time.

Meanwhile, he continued to work on a project begun in 1958, four years before *One Day in the Life* . . . was published. This was to be Solzhenitsyn's greatest contribution to his nation's literature—a modern history written in plain language rather than in the stilted jargon and corrupt distortions of official Soviet versions. His work would include a definitive exposé of the Soviet prison camp system, *The Gulag Archipelago*. Furthermore, Solzhenitsyn was determined that this writing would not be suppressed; somehow the history would be published and he would accept the consequences.

But in August 1973, the secret police gained access to a copy of the manuscript in circulation; a friend of the author committed suicide, and the machinery of Soviet cruelty began to put Solzhenitsyn on the rack. For months he lived in expectation of incarceration on trumped-up charges of lunacy. Only the vehement protests of the free Western press (acting, I believe, as agents of God's common grace to forestall the full fury of evil from doing its worst) prevented Solzhenitsyn's murder.

Living or dead, Aleksandr Solzhenitsyn exemplifies the final cost to be reckoned. For the writer whose sense of vocation transcends any lesser allegiance—and especially for the writer who, like Solzhenitsyn, is personally committed to belief in the One who is himself the Word-Made-Flesh—this high calling summons him to offer his entire being to God. Such a writer knows that his vocation is God's gift of grace extended by a loving Father; in return, the Father asks only that the writer take his gift and refine it into an art. Thus burnished and shining, the writer's art may then be offered back to God as sacrifice, service, and sacrament. But such an offering may be given only at a cost of spiritual affirmation free from compromise, a commitment, in Eliot's phrase, "costing not less than everything."

By contrast, James Joyce's young artist Stephen Dedalus wished "to live, to err, to fall, to triumph, to recreate life out of life"—but all in a spirit of rejection, for to succeed in his vision of flight beyond mundane concerns, Stephen felt compelled to reject home, country, and church. To free himself for his art, he utters the artist's most crippling denial: "I will not serve." Thereby Stephen Dedalus and all who follow his example condemn themselves to the isolation of the rejected self. For the true artist not only serves but, if necessary, also suffers. He suffers for what he believes, and he finds his richest reward when, through the authenticity of his representation of truth, others learn to appropriate his faith for themselves.

The great modern French novelist and Nobel laureate François Mauriac has told us,

> My writings have benefited from the fact that, no matter how lazy I was, I always wrote the least article with care, putting my whole soul into it.

The cost of being a writer is this commitment to excellence and integrity. But for the writer who professes to be a Christian, there is a surcharge to be paid. This is the call to sacrifice, service, and sacrament—a recognition that in using the medium of language, we are in fact employing symbolic representations of the Living Word. Surely this is why, at a school educating Christians for service—at a college or seminary—the most important courses are not those in systematic theology and apologetics, but in the study of words and the Word. Andre Gide may not have been what we would call an orthodox Christian, but he spoke with great insight when he prayed,

> O Lord, it is not because I have been told that you were the Son of God that I listen to your word; but your word is beautiful beyond any human word, and that is how I recognize that you are the Son of God.

Because Jesus Christ is the Living Word, we shall need to learn what the Scriptures tell us about him. But because he has given us, as it were, a part of himself—our very means of verbal expression—we are responsible to use language as a keenly sharpened tool. We are responsible to speak and write with precision, clarity, power, and illumination. We cannot be content until, as Eliot notes, we reach the stage described in this parenthesis:

> (where every word is at home,
> Taking its place to support the others,
> The word neither diffident nor ostentatious,
> An easy commerce of the old and the new,
> The common word exact without vulgarity,
> The formal word precise but not pedantic,
> The complete consort dancing together)

To reach this level of maturity, a writer must be patient. Emile Cailliet has said,

> As every writer worth his salt very well knows, there is only one specific, irreplaceable term that fits into a certain situation. It is the knack of hitting upon such terms continually, often by dint of laborious effort, which distinguishes the great stylist and helps dress the truth in beautiful garb. And this is, properly, the function of the artist.

Not only the function of the artist, but also the obligation of the Christian.

Jacques Maritain has written, "It is not easy to be a poet, it is not easy to be a Christian, it is doubly difficult to be both at once." No Christian who contemplates the vocation of writer should underestimate the cost; otherwise, as Jesus said in his parable, "all the onlookers will laugh at him" (Luke 14:29).

What does it cost to be a writer? Ultimately, the price must be an act of martyrdom, the daily laying down of one's life for the sake of the gospel. God has never been pleased by the cheap offerings of Cain. It remains one of the mysteries of faith that losing should be the only way to find, and dying the only way to live. What we keep back for ourselves atrophies, corrodes, and corrupts; what we give to others and to God becomes acceptable to the One in whose praise we offer it.

Yet, as with any vocation's fulfillment, the writer knows great rewards. To Jesus of Nazareth, the Roman centurion at Capernaum sent this message: "You need only say the word" (Matthew 8:8). *Say the Word!* To us who know him by name and honor him as Lord, Jesus Christ passes on that same commission. We are to say the Word, write the Word, live the Word.

How, then, can any cost be too great?

Ambidextrous Artists

My purpose in this book has been to show that each of us is called by God to the vocation of artist, since being made in the image of God entitles each human being to image forth the Creator. One way to fulfill our calling is by participating in the so-called fine arts—music, painting, poetry, drama, dance, sculpture, and the rest. But any discussion of Vocation that treats only the "fine arts" and ignores what are sometimes patronizingly called the "useful arts" is shortsighted. These skills and crafts include government, medicine, agriculture, manufacturing, and education. They are essential to our well-being as individuals and as members of human societies. In the New Testament letters, the Apostle Paul includes the divine gifts of teaching, helpfulness, and administration along with the supposedly more sanctified gifts of apostleship and prophecy. So, in our experience, we come to realize that we are ministered to by various callings. For while the fine arts hint at something like the eternal splendor of the New Jerusalem, the useful arts make it possible for us to fulfill our destiny here and now as guardians of our planet.

Furthermore, God places no restrictions or limitations on the form our art takes; God's only requirement is that whatever we offer be the best work of our hands. There are no explicitly "Christian" avenues of service. In fact, one of the paradoxes of our experience as Christians wishing to serve God is this: The more "spiritual" we become, the less effective seems to be our witness among those who know nothing but the tedium of secular existence. On the other hand, the more we know of physical labor and perspiration, comradeship and disappointment, love and loss; the closer we grow to the soil and to those soiled by life's vicissitudes; the deeper we probe the recesses of human fear and aspiration—in short, the greater our joy both in being human and in knowing who made us so—then and only then are we enough like Christ himself to perceive how best to devote our gift to his glory.

This may be tough meat for some Christians with baby teeth, especially if they've never been weaned from devotional primers. It's probably just as hard on saints with dentures! A good antidote to an overdose of ethereality is this passage from St. Paul's Second Letter to the Christians at Corinth.

> In order that our service may not be brought into discredit, we avoid giving offence in anything. As God's servants, we try to recommend ourselves in all circumstances by our steadfast endurance: in distress, hardships, and dire straits; flogged, imprisoned, mobbed; overworked, sleepless, starving. We recommend ourselves by the innocence of our behaviour, our grasp of truth, our patience and kindliness; by gifts of the Holy Spirit, by sincere love, by declaring the truth, by the power of God. We wield the weapons of righteousness in right hand and left. Honour and dishonour, praise and blame, are alike our lot: we are the impostors who speak the truth, the unknown men whom all men know; dying we still live on; disciplined by suffering, we are not done to death; in our sorrows we have always cause for joy; poor ourselves, we bring wealth to many; penniless, we own the world (2 Corinthians 6:3-10).

Throughout the New Testament, the metaphor of the soldier recurs. St. Paul tells Timothy, "Take your share of
hardship, like a good soldier of Christ Jesus" (2 Timothy
2:3). We are given to understand that the enemies against
whom we fight are spiritual powers; to oppose them, we
are urged to "put on all the armour which God provides,"
including the "helmet" of salvation and "the shield of
faith." With these and other battle dress to protect us, we
are to take up the "sword" of the Spirit (Ephesians 6:10-
17).

The terms of this figure of speech are entirely conventional. That is why, perhaps, I am struck with interest by a
phrase in St. Paul's description of his ministry among the
Corinthians: "We wield the weapons of righteousness in
right hand and left." In the context of the military
metaphor, one can argue that Paul refers simply to the
sword and shield, weapons customarily carried in the right
and left hands respectively—the sword for offense, the
shield for defense. So it may be; but is it possible that Paul
may have something entirely different in mind? Is it possible that Paul is calling for unconventional warfare by unconventional soldiers—for unconventional service by unconventional Christians? If so, then I am reminded of a
phrase from Søren Kierkegaard, who speaks of a need for
Christians to be "spies for God."

Consider for a moment some of the ramifications of
right- and left-handedness. Here we have a cosmopolitan
writer—a Greek-speaking Roman citizen of the Mediterra-
nean world; at the same time, he is very much a Middle
Eastern Jew, steeped in the customs and conventions of
oriental culture. Throughout that culture, the right hand
holds both symbolic and literal preeminence over the left.
Right-handedness is considered normal, usual, traditional;
to be right-handed is to be orthodox, conservative, obvious.

These same attitudes have carried down to our own times. When we wish to speak of reliability, we refer to someone as our *right-hand* man. When a hostess seats her guests at a formal dinner table, the guest of honor takes his place at her *right*. The patriarch Jacob had twelve sons, the youngest of whom was his favorite: his name was Benjamin, which means "the son of my right hand." Christians believe that in his exalted state, the Son of God, Jesus Christ, is seated at the right hand of the Father.

We greet each other—friends or total strangers—by extending to them our right hand; we induct new members into the church by welcoming them with "the right hand of fellowship." The custom derives from the ancient desire to show another warrior that we have come to him unarmed: there is no sword in our hand. Thus, the right hand is proffered with honor and integrity. Similarly, in a court of law the clerk or bailiff swears us to an oath, to "tell the truth, the whole truth, and nothing but the truth," by requiring us to raise the right hand. We distinguish between correct and incorrect behavior by referring to *right* and wrong. We specify a person's sanity by asking if he is in his *right* mind. It's all so familiar to us, we often take quite for granted the significance of the right hand in our lives and language.

But while the right hand signifies all these honored and acceptable states, the left hand is always suspect and treated with either alarm or contempt. If you are left-handed, you have probably suffered from lack of consideration or neglect on the part of an essentially right-handed world. You have sat at school desks whose tablet arm is on the right side; you have written in notebooks whose spiral ring cuts into your left wrist. The same is true of scissors and commercial coffeepots and a host of other items put together by thoughtless right-handers.

But these indignities to lefties are at least benign. In

ancient times, someone with left-handed tendencies was assumed to be possessed by evil, probably in cahoots with Satan. The Latin word for "left" tells it all: *sinister*. The French have maintained the prejudice, although we use their word *gauche* as a synonym for "clumsy" or "socially tactless" rather than as a reference to evil. Still, to be left-handed is considered odd; in fact, one suggestion attributes left-handedness to a birth defect—brain damage resulting in this congenital deformity. Perhaps that's carrying the bias too far; certainly, however, there is no escaping the pejorative connotations in left-handedness: unorthodox, radical, even devious. And in Asia especially, there is one thing more: the left hand is impure and socially unacceptable. In the East, never—under any circumstances—may one be permitted the typical Western custom when shaking hands, the effusive gesture of gripping his arm with your left hand or in any other way touching him with your left hand. The left hand must never be used to handle your own food or to pass a dish to anyone at your table. Why? Because in those Asian countries where there is no toilet paper, the left hand serves that purpose.

Even with all these connotations and customs before him, the Apostle Paul may be urging Christians to violate convention, to do the unexpected—in short, to be ambidextrous, using both right hand and left hand for Jesus Christ. It is clear from other Scripture, of course, that God needs those who can serve him in unusual ways. The Book of Judges, for instance, gives us two examples.

Do you remember Ehud, of whom we read in Judges 3? The Israelites had been subjected to the tyranny of Eglon, king of Moab, for eighteen years. But the Lord raised up a deliverer—a devious, left-handed assassin named Ehud. The narrator tells us his story in rich detail and irony. As an apparently dutiful subject, Ehud prepares a gift of tribute to the oppressor-king Eglon. This bloated obscenity of a man is seated on the roof of his summer palace when Ehud is ushered into his presence. But in addition to the gift he bears, Ehud also carries under his clothes a dagger much shorter than the usual sword; furthermore, because Ehud is left-handed, he wears it on his right hip.

When Ehud presents himself, the king's guards frisk him in the usual manner, looking for a weapon on the left side, where any normal soldier wears his sword. Finding nothing there, they admit him, and Ehud offers his gift. Then he gives Eglon an enigmatic message: "I have a word from the Lord for you" (Judges 3:20). The king dismisses his courtiers and guards to hear the prophecy in private. When they are alone, Ehud whips out his concealed dagger and plunges it into Eglon's belly so that—we read in the vivid language of the King James Version—"the haft also went in after the blade; and the fat closed upon the blade, so that he could not draw the dagger out of his belly; and the dirt came out" (Judges 3:22). Ehud leaves the fallen Eglon quietly, and when he returns to his own people he summons them to a great victory over the Moabites—all because he used his left-handedness for God.

In another passage, we are told about 700 southpaw slingers who could aim at a target and not miss "by a hair's breadth" (Judges 20:15, 16). Their accuracy, of course, is an asset; so too the element of surprise produced by their unorthodox sliders. The enemy expects a slinger's stone to curve in one direction; instead, these stones, thrown by left-handers, come at a different angle.

But even more useful than these left-handed warriors is a group of sharpshooters in David's army. These valiant commandos, on the run from the vengeful King Saul, were expert slingers and archers; furthermore, they were ambidextrous, able to "sling stones and shoot arrows with the left hand or the right" (1 Chronicles 12:2). To the soldier fighting his battles in the badlands of the Judaean wilderness—hiding behind boulders, peering through a crack in the cave's entrance—what an advantage to be able to attack with either hand! What a loss to have to give up a shot because the left hand is too weak or unskilled to use at the best angle of vision.

For a basketball player it is the same. Watch Julius Erving or Phil Ford in a driving layup. A head feint to the right, a step to the left, and he is airborne, leaving his defender to wonder whether the ball will come from the right or left side. The element of surprise—the ability to keep opponents off balance—is what makes these athletes formidable.

In choosing the twelve apostles, Jesus Christ knew the value of balancing right- and left-handedness. He called a political conservative, a member of the Israeli freedom fighters identified as the Zealot Party, a man known to his intimates as Simon Zelotes, Simon the Zealot. He was part of an intensely nationalistic conspiracy committed to violent revolt against Rome, opposing any concession to Rome's authority, especially for the purposes of taxation. The Zealots were fifth columnists, trained as guerrillas, experts in underground warfare.

Simon's diametric political opposite is Matthew the tax-collector. As a hated publican, Matthew represents to Simon the Zealot everything he is fighting to drive out of Israel. Matthew stands for peace at any price; he is an opportunist, enriching himself with his levies on behalf of the Emperor against his own countrymen. Matthew is a collaborator with the enemy, a quisling, a fink.

Imagine these two men in the same congregation or on the same college faculty today! One is a member of the John Birch Society; the other, Americans for Democratic Action. One sympathizes with James J. Kilpatrick; the other admires Shana Alexander. One opposes giving away the American canal in Panama; the other is embarrassed by our lingering neocolonialism. One insists that the United Nations Organization be expelled from American soil; the other laments that so few evangelicals support the UN's resolutions against oppression and racism. What a world of difference between them! Yet Jesus calls both Simon and Matthew into the first community of Christians. To Simon, the political right-winger, he says, "Love your enemies." To Matthew, the political leftist, he says, "Pray for those who persecute you." To both of them, Jesus says, "Follow me, . . . for I have not come to call the righteous, but sinners." Jesus Christ takes their differences and—in spite of everything that would seem to drive Simon and Matthew apart—brings them into unity of purpose; then Jesus uses each of them in the uniqueness of his individual traits and temperament.

"We wield the weapons of righteousness in right hand and left," says St. Paul. The Scriptures bear out the validity of inferring ambidextrous service for Christ from this military metaphor. Soldiers, athletes, politicians—whichever side they favor—are all called to serve. But if it is true that "the pen is mightier than the sword," then the call for ambidextrous soldiers of Christ must also be a summons to writers and other artists who would wield the pen, the chisel, the brush, in right hand and left.

In a 1977 talk given at Canterbury Cathedral, Lord Kenneth, Clark of Saltwood, whose television lectures have educated millions to the meaning of *civilization*, remarked that "the art of our own day used in the service of the Church has lost much of its power to move us either as lovers of art or as Christians." He observed that art, as most Christians experience it, is either "artistically an anachronism, bearing no relation to the living art of our time," or else it is "self-consciously arty, bearing no relation to the needs of worshipers." Fearing to "strike out into the controversial wilderness of modern art," Lord Clark says, most Christians decide to settle for the old-fashioned in music or painting or stained glass because it is safe and familiar; consequently, we end up with "the convenient second-rate." Not so the great architects and builders of the Middle Ages, for as Lord Clark reminds us, their cathedrals demonstrate that "everything done for the glory of God should be the finest and most splendid which the mind of man could devise or his hand execute."

Instead of parroting old standards and issuing imitations derived from somebody else's model, artists who are Christians ought to recognize that Jesus Christ isn't interested in how much we sound like Andrae Crouch or Norma Zimmer; he isn't concerned with whether or not we write like C. S. Lewis or Elisabeth Elliot. Jesus Christ wants us to serve him with the full range of our own talents. He calls us to exercise the imagination given to every individual; he calls us to find our own style, to know ourselves well enough to set down our own mode of expression. To do this consistently and well, we need to be at the cutting edge of each day's new experience, living as it were even on the brink of absurdity. Today's challenges and confrontations should transform our art to exemplify the fact that we are living life with a purpose fulfilling itself day by day. To serve Jesus Christ as an artist means offering to my Lord something that nobody else in the whole universe can give him—my own particular gift.

This magnificent truth has never been more powerfully expressed than by the poet Gerard Manley Hopkins in his sonnet, "As kingfishers catch fire." By illustrating with birds, insects, stones, and bells, the poet shows how

> Each mortal thing does one thing and the same:
> namely, to be *itself* and nothing more,
> Crying *What I do is me: for that I came.*

But then Hopkins reaches beyond particularity of natural objects to treat the special responsibilities of human individuals. Here, as a Christian, the poet finds support in the theology of the Incarnation. If every other creature serves God by being itself, so too must human beings. But human beings have also an added dimension. We are rightly ourselves; but because of the Incarnation, each of us—says Hopkins—

> Acts in God's eye what in God's eye he is—
> Christ.

As believers in Jesus Christ, you and I have not only been indwelt by the Spirit of God; we have also become incarnate representatives to God of his dearly beloved Son. Therefore, the gift we offer back to God is ourselves, reshaped from our brokenness to be in the image and likeness of Christ himself. For, as the poet concludes,

> . . . Christ plays in ten thousand places,
> Lovely in limbs, and lovely in eyes not his
> To the Father through the features of men's faces.

Too often our art is not only cheap and derivative, but also predictable. The world has grown entirely too accustomed to our methods of proclamation; the world knows exactly what to expect from our dull routines, our cycles of sameness, the clichés by which we presume to transmit the splendor of the gospel. Yet every so often we are stunned by the unusual, which only serves to highlight how static and stagnant our imaginations have become.

On a recent visit to Scotland Lory, our daughter Ellyn, and I toured the famous Glamis Castle, childhood home of the Queen Mother Elizabeth and legendary scene of Duncan's murder by Macbeth. In the castle is a small family chapel with walls and ceiling decorated by panels depicting the twelve apostles and scenes from the life of Christ. This work was done by the seventeenth-century Dutch limner Jan de Wet, who also painted the portraits of Scotland's kings for the Palace of Holyrood in Edinburgh. In most respects, de Wet's work is typical of his Dutch tradition. But one of his illustrations almost leaps off the wall, so compelling is this artist's imagination.

The scene shows Mary Magdalene in the burial garden, having just recognized the Risen Lord. She kneels with arms upraised and hands open, about to touch him. Many such paintings exist; viewing them, one wonders why—even in grief—Mary should not have been able to recognize Jesus at sight, as John 20:14 records. But de Wet's painting differs from all others and helps us to understand Mary's confusion. For the figure of Christ stands in the foreground looking precisely like any good Dutch burgher—wearing a large, broad-brimmed, black hat and leaning on a shovel! Seeing a picture of Jesus in a hat is strange enough, but as we stare in shock at the tool he carries, we recall these words:

> At this, she turned around and saw Jesus standing there, but she did not realize that it was Jesus.
>
> "Woman," he said, "why are you crying? Who is it you are looking for?"
>
> Thinking he was the gardener, she said, "Sir, if you have carried him away, tell me where you have put him, and I will get him."
>
> Jesus said to her, "Mary" (John 20:14-16, *New International Version*).

By his refusal to be content with the usual, de Wet's painting illumines the Evangelist's text and sets an example for every other artist.

The world has also become complacent about its own casual attitudes toward evil. Today we need Christians as artists who can take the world by surprise. The late Flannery O'Connor, fiction writer and apologist for the Christian faith, put the challenge in these terms:

> The novelist with Christian concerns will find in modern life distortions which are repugnant to him, and his problem will be to make these appear as distortions to an audience which is used to seeing them as natural; and he may well be forced to take ever more violent means to get his vision across to this hostile audience.

Then she went on to say,

> When you can assume that your audience holds the same beliefs you do, you can relax a little and use more normal ways of talking to it; when you have to assume that it does not, then you have to make your vision apparent by shock— to the hard of hearing you shout, and for the almost blind you draw large and startling figures.

Jesus of Nazareth himself was unconventional; he stood out from the rest, so much so that the midnight inquirer Nicodemus noted the young rabbi's distinctiveness. Jesus defied the expectations of those who looked for conformity; he literally overturned the categories of their thinking; he would not allow himself to be forced into their box. Jesus was free, free as the wind that blows first from the north, then from south, from east or from west, as it wishes. That's the freedom he offers to everyone born again by the Spirit, a freedom to be right- or left-handed, to come from whichever direction the Breath of God blows you.

This is still dangerous teaching in some quarters, but thank God, there is increasing freedom within the Church for Christians to serve Jesus Christ in unconventional ways. In 1949, when Billy Graham held his tent meetings in Los Angeles and word began filtering out that movie stars and other entertainment personalities were identifying themselves with Jesus Christ, two reactions were common. First, disbelief that their professions of faith could be sincere; second, an unqualified expectation that if these conversions meant anything, Hollywood would become a ghost town as actors and other artists gave up their careers. There was no thought among evangelicals that a Christian could act, dance, sing, or otherwise corrupt himself in show business.

Today we know of an ongoing witness for Jesus Christ among actors and designers, opera or country-music singers, concert pianists and trumpet players. There are believers making their faith known in television and recordings, in films and on stage. For them, the way is far from easy because the very fame that gives their witness its wide influence sears with its spotlight and heightens any blemish to their testimony. Gossip-mongers enjoy publicizing any defectors from the faith, show business personalities whose loudly acclaimed announcement of being "born again" collapses like the house built upon sand— and great is the fall thereof! But an artist is the same as any other Christian: Not perfect, just forgiven, as the slogan says. For spiritual growth and nurture toward maturity, some of these professionals have aligned with organizations such as the Fellowship of Christians in the Arts, Media, and Entertainment. Like their fellow-believers, the professional athletes who meet for worship and Bible study in hotels or in the locker rooms of great arenas, the entertainers have learned that a building doesn't have to have a steeple to house the Church of Jesus Christ.

In 1977, other professional artists organized themselves at a conference held on the campus of Bethel College. They call themselves "Christians Involved with the Visual Arts"—a nucleus of painters, potters, sculptors, and photographers desiring to find encouragement to go on with their art as a God-inspired vocation. Still another group recently banded together, calling itself "Fellowship of Artists in Cultural Evangelism." Convinced that cross-cultural evangelism can be enhanced by the Church's awareness of the power of art to speak its own symbolic language, this Fellowship seeks to develop the vocation of artist into a ministry recognized in mission priorities.

One such missionary endeavor, according to Bill Cole of Light Records, is a witness to unbelievers in the secular music market. "We must reach out to the secular world and penetrate their awareness just as secular music has penetrated Christian awareness," says Cole. This, surely, is a difficult challenge to musicians and other Christians in their own medium; yet it is a challenge and a need we dare not ignore. Certainly no one can dispute the effect of such witness where it has been received—the late Mahalia Jackson's singing her Chicago gospel or the power in Johnny Cash and Tennessee Ernie Ford's music. And who could have predicted that a recording of John Newton's "Amazing Grace," sung by Judy Collins, would reach into so many lives?

I cannot neglect to mention here writers who keep to their calling, serving Jesus Christ by writing their essays and poems, novels and plays. At the risk of omitting some, I name only a few contemporaries: Edmund Fuller, literary critic for *The Wall Street Journal*; Madeleine L'Engle, author of prize-winning children's books; novelists Graham Greene and Alan Paton, John Updike and D. Keith Mano; and preeminently Aleksandr Solzhenitsyn, whose work reflects what the Russian poet Osip Mandelstam realized in his search to find the source of joy: The Christian's art is joyous because it is free, and it is free because Christ died to redeem the world. Since Christ has already accomplished redemption, the artist need not die to save the world; he has only "the blissful responsibility to enjoy the world."

St. Paul warns the ambidextrous Christian, however, not to anticipate being accepted, even among fellow-believers. The Christian must be a living contradiction to the prevailing secularism, a loving enemy of the world and its system of values; he must also be a critic of popular culture and comfortable religion. Unfortunately, other Christians may misunderstand our unconventional service. It's curious how often we jump to disallow what God has already approved. The voice that rebuked Simon Peter on the rooftop in Joppa still speaks the same message: "It is not for you to call profane what God counts clean" (Acts 10:15). Nevertheless, honor may be tainted by dishonor, praise by blame. The Christian's highest loyalty may seem like disloyalty; still, like the prophet Micaiah, the Christian must declare, "As the Lord lives, I will say only what the Lord tells me to say" (1 Kings 22:14). If some call the artist an impostor, so be it. Yet if his art points to Creation and Redemption through the Incarnation—the intersecting of history by "the timeless moment"—then is not the artist, like the Apostle Paul, an impostor who speaks the truth? And if so, there is no reason for us to lay aside our particular gift—the weapon wielded in right hand or left—just because a fellow-soldier finds he cannot use it!

A final word of caution: There's nothing superior about being either right-handed or left-handed. You may stand on a street corner giving out gospel tracts while your brother promotes a "Jesus Festival"; you may sing "When Morning Gilds the Skies" while your sister prefers "Morning Has Broken," as arranged by Cat Stevens. Neither means of service is more important to God than the other. Whether our service to Jesus Christ is conventional or unconventional doesn't really matter. What is important is that our witness be clear and unmistakable. The French novelist and playwright Albert Camus once said, "What the world expects of Christians is that Christians should speak out loud and clear, in such a way that never a doubt, never the slightest doubt, could rise in the heart of the simplest man."

You see, in the end, that's what it's really all about. Not winning Nobel Prizes or Oscars or Emmys; not selling a million records or a million books; not making a name for ourselves by competing, as T. S. Eliot says, with "men whom one cannot hope/ To emulate." No, it is none of this. Instead, says Eliot, "For us, there is only the trying. The rest is not our business." For at the end of time, when the Lord himself calls us to account, what matters will not be our accomplishments, our splendid and prodigious achievements done in his name; what matters is whether or not we shall be able to say, "We are servants and deserve no credit; we have only done our duty" (Luke 17:10). Then indeed our art for God will glisten in the sunlight of his approval.